JAZZ LEAD GUITAR *Sol*

The Ultimate Guide to Playing Great Leads

CHRIS BUONO

Alfred, the leader in educational publishing,
and the National Guitar Workshop,
one of America's finest guitar schools, have joined
forces to bring you the best, most progressive
educational tools possible. We hope you will enjoy
this book and encourage you to look for
other fine products from Alfred and the
National Guitar Workshop.

ISBN 0-7390-3158-9 (Book & CD)

*This book was acquired, edited and produced
by Workshop Arts, Inc., the publishing arm of
the National Guitar Workshop.
Nathaniel Gunod: acquisitions, managing editor
Matthew Cramer: music typesetter and assistant editor
Timothy Phelps: interior design
CD Recorded at Monkey Boy Studios, New York, NY*

Cover photo: Jeff Oshiro

TABLE OF CONTENTS

A compact disc is included with this book. Using the CD will help make learning more enjoyable and the information more meaningful. The symbol below appears at the top of the first page of every solo. It will help you find the track on the CD.

With Solo, Track 00
Backing Track, Track 01

The CD provides recordings of the author performing the solos in this book and backing tracks for you to practice with. Track 1 will help you tune to the CD.

Have fun!

Chris Buono is an active bandleader and sideman in New York. Chris has performed and recorded in a variety of styles including modern jazz and jazz/funk, rock, world music, and the avant-garde throughout the eastern United States, Canada and abroad. His unique playing style can be heard on numerous major and independent label releases, some of which have received airplay on national radio and television. Chris has been teaching privately since 1993 and holds a bachelor's degree in Music Studies from William Paterson University. He also teaches for the National Guitar Workshop and the Toms River Music Academy in New Jersey.

For details, please visit www.chrisbuono.com.

Acknowledgements

My deepest thanks goes to my wife, my one and only, and my son for undying love and support and an endless supply of inspiration.

Special thanks go out to the following cast of truly amazing people: Rodney Holmes, Bill Foster, Arne Wendt and Zen Zadrovich for their great playing and good company; Brad Albetta and Brain Fulk at Monkey Boy Studios in New York for their expertise and patience; Jason Acuna at Acuna-Patada Studios in New Jersey and his wonderful family for their generosity; Tony C. and Kyle Kelso for their colossal act of kindness; Dave Smolover, Paula Abate and Nat Gunod for having faith in me and giving me the opportunity to write this book; Doug Osborn, Steve Hager, Connor McCarthy and Bob Lanzetti for their excellent and speedy transcriptions; David "Fuze" Fiuczynski for confidence, support and great friendship since day one.

Thanks always to: the entire Buono, D'Alessio and Lordi families; John Clarizio; Tony Palmucci; Frankie Cicala; Gerry Carboy; Vic Juris; and Wayne Krantz.

This book is dedicated to Louis V. Buono, Sr., John Cacopardo, and Joseph Renda.

Jazz Lead Guitar Solos is for the rock or blues guitarist who wants to walk a day in the life of a jazz cat. The content of this book is all about one thing: learning how to play great jazz guitar solos! It teaches by example, providing eight complete solos for you to learn. These solos, in various jazz styles, are accompanied by lessons describing the tools used to create them and explanations of the chord progressions they were played over. Also included are real-life lessons presented in a direct, yet fun format on subjects that go to the very essence of playing jazz.

This book is meant for guitarists who, having attained an intermediate level, desire to broaden their musical vocabulary. To get the most out of the material, the reader should have experience playing lead guitar and be familiar with the following:

- Reading a chord chart or lead sheet with chord symbols
- Reading standard music notation, guitar tablature, chord and scale diagrams
- Reading in different key signatures
- Intermediate theory, including the major scale, the relative minor, the different types of minor scales and the modes of the major scale (Dorian, Mixolydian, and so on)
- Chord extensions and alterations
- Diatonic harmony and Roman numeral analysis (for example you should know what *ii–V–I* means)
- Basic chord progressions, such as the 12-bar blues
- Using scales to play lead guitar solos

This is neither a technique manual nor a theory book. It is about the concepts that are important to building a good jazz solo. It takes a broad look at a vast array of topics essential to jazz soloing, and should be used as a starting point from which to continue learning about the subject. The concepts covered are not exclusive to jazz soloing, and you will find them helpful with other styles that involve improvisation, such as rock and blues. For a thorough study of jazz guitar, check out *The Complete Jazz Guitar Method* by Jody Fisher.

Jazz is music of the moment, and there's no better to way to learn how to play in the moment than to actually *look* at the moment on paper. The music you'll hear on the accompanying CD is *real*. These are not prewritten exercises or rehearsed songs. The solos were actually improvised and then transcribed note-for-note for you to look over. This way, you don't have go to your local concert hall and continually stop the band so that you can question them about, say, how to use the altered scale. It's all right here.

Jazz is not all that hard to play, but learning to do it will require discipline and dedicated practice. Hopefully, this book will answer a lot of questions you were afraid to ask, and eliminate any fears you might have had about playing jazz and improvising over chord changes. Most of all, I hope you'll find real enjoyment in working up some jazz chops.

Have fun!

The solos and their lessons have been put in a progressive order—starting at a fairly easy level and becoming more difficult—and should be studied in the order given. Each new concept presented within a solo and its lessons can be found in the next solo. As you progress, it would be a good idea to review earlier lessons and observe how previously learned concepts show up in the more difficult solos

Here's how each chapter in the book is organized:

The Chart

This section will have a *chart* (musical score) showing the chords over which the solo was played. Try to look at this chart while listening to the CD so that you really hear the "story" being told before you dive into learning to play the solo from the transcription. Later in the book, this section will often include a basic *head* (melody).

The Solo Transcription

The next section is the bread and butter: the solos. They're transcribed here in standard notation and tablature for you to analyze and, of course, play. Though it is not necessary for you to know how to read music to be a great lead guitarist, thoroughly understanding some of the material will require that you are at least able to recognize and understand the rhythms in the standard notation.

Because of the complex rhythmic communication amongst the members of a band, and more importantly, the soloist's *feel* and *phrasing,* the rhythms of transcribed jazz solos are often *quantized* (adjusted) to the nearest logical note values. Remember, jazz is a music of the moment and these improvised solos were recorded live with some burnin' players, so none of the transcriptions are 100 percent exact.

The Tools of the Trade

In this section you get the information needed to start sounding "jazzy." There are explanations of the materials used to build the solo, fingerings for the scales, and so on. This section will help you build your jazz vocabulary. Also included are matching chord voicings so you can start to visualize the areas of the fretboard in which to play. All of this information will help you learn to hear and see the big picture.

The scales are oriented horizontally, like this:

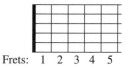

Frets: 1 2 3 4 5

Chords are oriented vertically, like this: ⟶

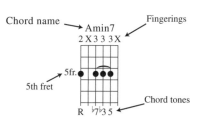

If a chord or scale is played in the open position, the nut is represented with a heavy black line. In chord diagrams, fret numbers are not given in open position.

The Real Deal

This last section contains concepts that you will need to know to pass as a jazz cat. The ideas are presented in a relaxed format and will give you the real-life skinny about building a great jazz solo and just being a jazzer.

Horizontal vs. Vertical

You will see the terms *horizontal* and *vertical* used frequently in this book, so be sure to read this page. Understanding the lessons in this book will require knowing the concepts described by these terms.

When improvising lines in lead guitar solos, there are two different approaches:

Horizontal

A horizontal approach is when your lines are derived from one scale that works across several harmonies. An example you can probably relate to is when you first learned to improvise over the 12-bar blues progression using the minor pentatonic scale. You had three chord changes thrown at you in twelve measures and you learned to play licks from the one scale "across" all three of those changes. This is horizontal improvisation.

Vertical

A vertical approach involves a little more thinking at first. When you improvise vertically, you're playing melodic ideas from one or more source (scale, arpeggio, etc.) over each individual chord. Going back to the 12-bar blues example, instead of streaming across the changes with the one minor pentatonic scale, you would play a different minor pentatonic scale over each of the three chords. This would be vertical improvisation. Jazz cats often call this "making the changes."

Horizontal playing probably comes naturally to you. The goal is to sound as natural with vertical playing as you do with horizontal playing.

Swing 8ths

Swing eighth notes are often described as a triplet figure where the first two eighth notes are tied together. This figure lends the music a bouncy or swinging feel.

Swinging the time also has a lot to do with the use of accents and *dynamics* (loudness and softness) within the phrase. The forward motion that swing possesses is a result of accenting particular notes, controlled use of varied dynamics, strong use of syncopated rhythms, and even, *legato* note values (giving each note its full value, connecting the notes). Your concept of swing feel will also develop by constant listening to recordings and lots of specific practice.

All of the eighth notes in this book should be swung unless otherwise indicated with the direction *Straight 8ths*,

Now let's play!

Solo 1

The Chart

"Blues for My One and Only" is a slow, three-*chorus* (each repetition of a progression is called a chorus) 12-bar minor blues progression in the key of G Minor. Because the basic blues progression uses few chords, it is a good place to begin exploring jazz soloing. Also, the slow tempo gives you time to relax and just play. These changes can be found in many jazz tunes, notably John Coltrane's haunting blues in C Minor, "Equinox."

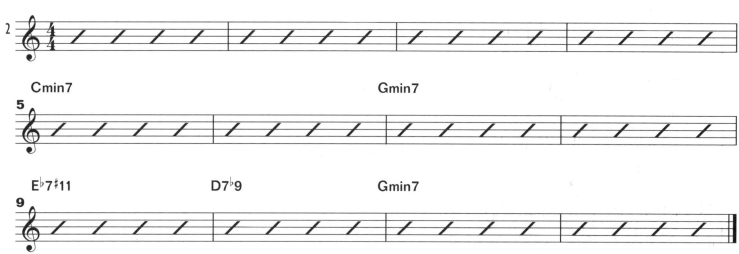

- Remember that the chordal instrument that's accompanying you will use extensions (9, 11 and 13) and altered chord tones (♭5, ♯5, ♭9, ♯9, ♯11 and ♭13) with these chords to enhance the overall sound, and, more important, interact with the lines you are playing.

- Notice the distinctive E7♯11–D7♭9–Gmin7 (♭VI–V7–i) *turnaround* (an ending that leads back to the beginning, sometimes used as an introduction) at bars 9–12. This minor blues turnaround is unique sounding and interesting to play over.

Blues for My One and Only Transcription

Transcribed by Bob Lanzetti

♩ = 110

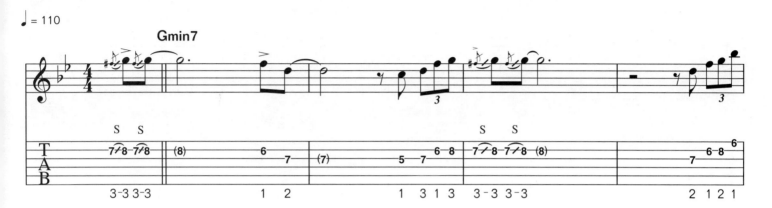

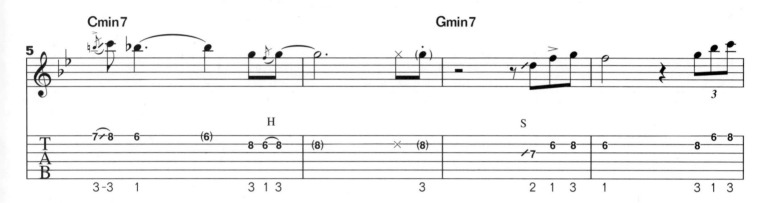

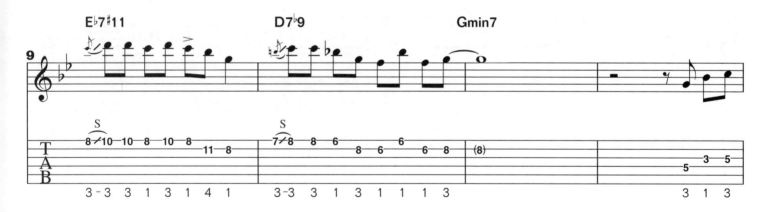

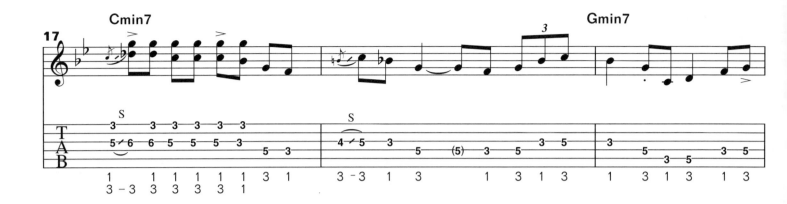

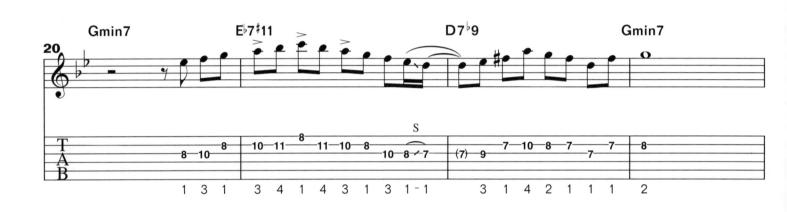

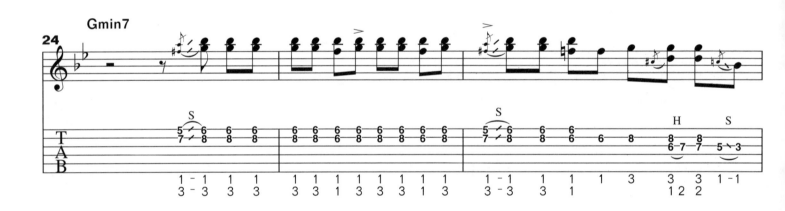

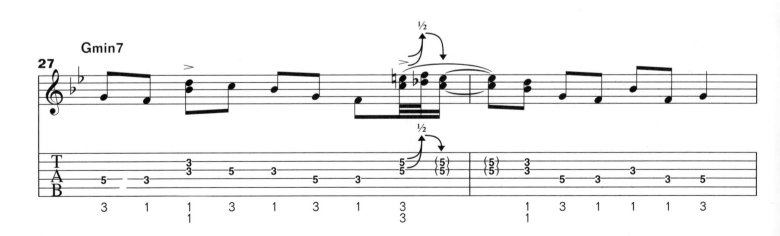

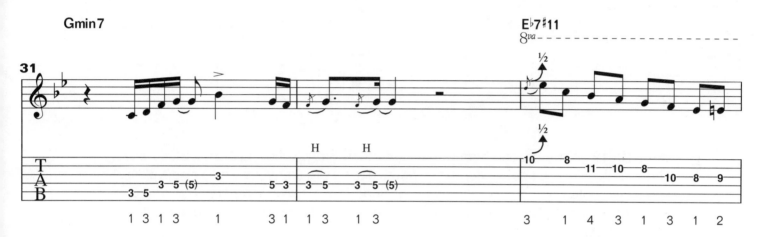

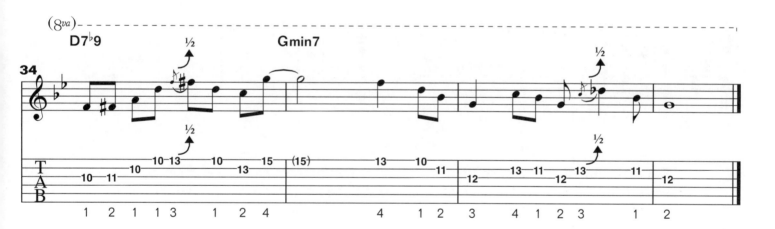

8va = *Ottava alta.* Play an octave higher than written.

This *5th-position* (four to six fret area starting at the 5th fret) G Minor Pentatonic scale did the job for a horizontal approach to the entire first chorus, **bars 1–12**. Notice that the scale formula is shown between the music and TAB in the examples that follow. The numbers compare the minor pentatonic scale degrees to those of a major scale, which are as follows: 1–2–3–4–5–6–7–8(1). If a note in the minor pentatonic scale is a half step lower than that of the major scale, a flat ♭ precedes the number name. For example, 3 in the G Major scale is the note B, so the B♭ in the G Minor Pentatonic scale is called ♭3. This is called a *parallel major comparison*, and it is how all the scales in this book are explained.

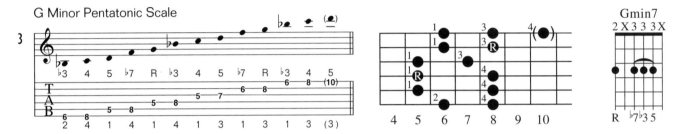

G Minor Pentatonic Scale

Bars 13–19 of the second chorus use the stock 3rd position G Minor Blues scale shown below for the *double stops* (two notes played simultaneously by a single player) and single-note lines. The double stops were performed with *hybrid picking*: The 3rd-string notes were played with the pick and the 1st-string notes were played with the right-hand middle finger.

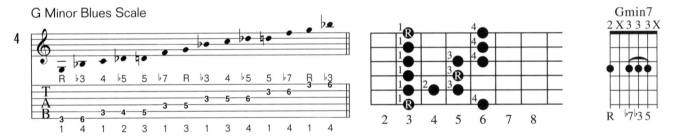

G Minor Blues Scale

Bars 21 and 22 of the second chorus employ two one-octave scales. This type of scale fingering is very useful in vertically approached playing over changes in which roots are close together, such as the E♭7♯11 and D7♭9 chords in these measures. Bar 21 uses the 8th-position E♭ Lydian Dominant scale, while bar 22 uses the 7th-position D Mixolydian scale.

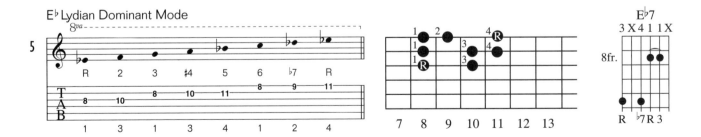

E♭ Lydian Dominant Mode

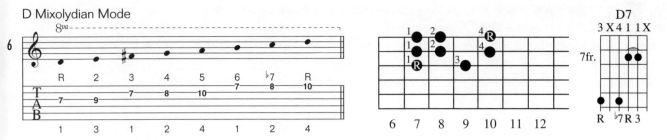

D Mixolydian Mode

Bar 24 leads into the third and final chorus with the 5t-position G Minor pentatonic scale used in the entire first chorus (see page 12). The line continues to go down to the 3rd-position G Minor Pentatonic scale with an added major 6th degree, which is used for the double-stop bend in **bar 27**, giving this a bluesy, *Dorian* (1–2–♭3–4–5–6–♭7) sound.

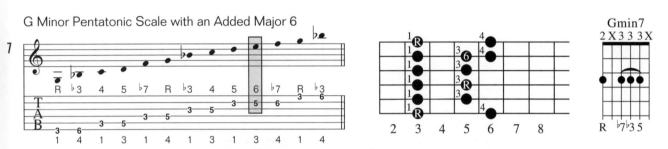

G Minor Pentatonic Scale with an Added Major 6

A vertical approach over the IV chord in **bars 29 and 30** results in the use of the 3rd-position C Minor Pentatonic scale shown below. Using two different scales in the same position for two different chords creates a smoother transition from one vertical idea to another. In this case, we are changing from the 3rd-position G Minor Pentatonic to the 3rd-position C Minor Pentatonic.

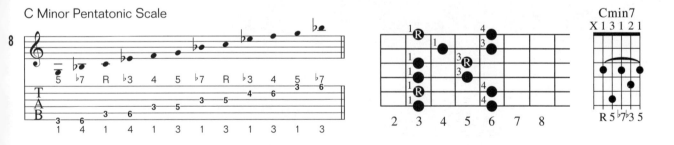

C Minor Pentatonic Scale

Enharmonic Respellings

When two notes have different names but sound at the same pitch they are called *enharmonic equivalents*. It is common for notes to be enharmonically respelled for the sake of easier reading (reducing the number of accidentals in a measure). For example, the ♭5 of a blues scale may be spelled as a ♯4 , thus making a natural sign ♮ for a natural 5 later in the measure unnecessary. There are many examples of this in the solo transcriptions in this book.

Bar 33 finds us back in the 8th-position E♭ Lydian Dominant one-octave scale shown on page 12, but this time the D7 arpeggio below is used in **bar 34** to bring the D7♭9 home to the *tonic* chord, i, Gmin7. The tonic chord is the one built on the first degree of the scale.

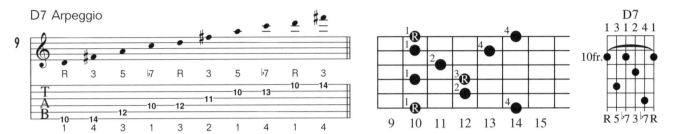

The final bluesy G Minor Pentatonic lick in **bars 35–37** uses the same fingering found in the C Minor Pentatonic scale used in bars 29 and 30 (page 13), but it has been moved up to the 10th position.

*The **John Coltrane** quartet of the 1960s were groundbreakers in the modal jazz movement going on at the time.*

Hipster's Dictionary

This is a guide to some common jazz terms and phrases you will see in this book or hear in real life. When you're ready to go and test out your new jazz guitar skills on the world, some of these words and phrases will surely come up, and with this guide, you will be a "hip jazz cat."

Bandstand: The stage on which will you dazzle the world with your future jazz chops.

Behind the beat: To intentionally slow down or "expand" the feel by playing a little after the beat.

Blowin': A term commonly used to describe the action of soloing.

Chart: Jazz slang for a musical score (written music).

Chorus: Once through the chord progression.

Comp: Short for ac*comp*any or *comp*lement. Usually used in describing the role of the piano or guitar player supporting your lead jazz guitar solo.

Downbeat: The first beat of a full measure.

Gig: The performance. The be all and end all, the playing field, the battleground, your livelihood, your home away from home, your reason for getting up every day and spending most of it hunched over a guitar, bobbing back and forth to a metronome, getting ready to tear the roof off with your jazz weaponry.

Head: The main melody of the tune.

Hip: A state of cool.

In the pocket: When playing in a group, the delicate art of rhythmically being where you need to be at all costs.

Lines: Jazz cat name for an improvised melody.

Out: The art of playing outside the key signature; or, where you will be in terms of the band if you constantly do this incorrectly night after night.

Scat: Improvisational jazz singing using nonsense syllables, such as: *doo–be–doo–wop, dop–a–famalama–jama, bo–de–do–sciddly–be–boo, ya–ya.*

Straight ahead: A style of jazz performed mostly on acoustic instruments that follows the traditional head-solos-head form and employs a conservative approach to composition and improvisation.

Superimposing: Playing a melodic idea from one harmony over another harmony.

Swingin': As in, "You are swingin'." The art of putting your notes in just the right spot.

Swing feel: Playing the eighth notes unevenly, long-short, something like an eighth-note triplet with the second eighth tied to the first. Also implies a certain kind of articulation, syncopation and accenting that must be learned by listening.

Train wreck: What happens when a fatal mistake is made on the bandstand and all is lost, such as blowin' a solo while someone else is playing the head and it's not even over the same changes.

Tritone sub: Short for *tritone substitution*. The hip act of replacing a chord with another chord whose root is a tritone (three whole steps) above. Usually done with dominant 7th chords, for example, replacing G7 with D♭7.

Tune: Jazz cat word for a song.

Turnaround: A series of chords that creates an ending that often leads back to the beginning, sometimes used as an introduction.

Two-beat ii–V: A ii–V progression where the ii and the V chord last two beats each.

Two-beat or **four-beat:** The difference between feeling a common time groove in *half* or *cut time* (two-beat), or the full four-beat pulse (four-beat).

Solo 2

The Chart

"Johnny B. Blues Thing" is another three-chorus, 12-bar blues progression. The main difference between this set of blues changes and "Blues for My One and Only" is that this one is a *major blues*: The dominant sound is heard in the I7 and IV7 chords. From Charlie Parker's "Billie's Bounce" to Thelonious Monk's "Straight, No Chaser," this chart has been used on countless jazz recordings and is a standard at any jam session.

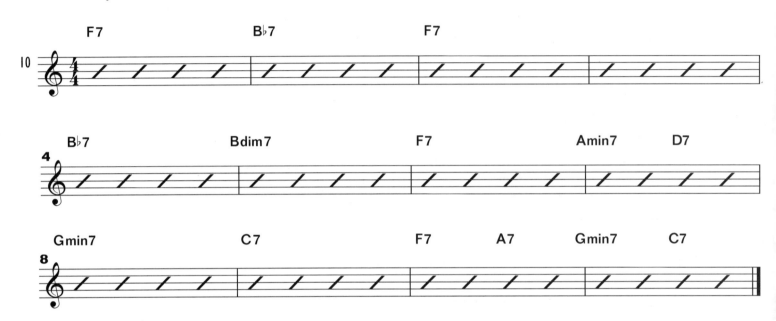

- Check out the always-cool #IV diminished 7th chord in bar 6.

- Take notice of the ii–Vs in **bars 8 and 12**.

- In **bars 9–12** we find the stock jazz-blues turnaround. More specifically, **bars 11** and **12** have the I–VI–ii–V7 turnaround that can be found in many other jazz and non-jazz styles. If there's one turnaround in this book that has to become second nature, this is it.

If you have studied diatonic harmony, you know that neither IV nor VI is dominant in the diatonic system (in a major key). In the blues, anything can be dominant. The dominant chord on VI is actually acting as a *secondary dominant*; that is, it is behaving as a V7 of the ii chord it precedes. This is a common practice in jazz, so if it is unfamiliar to you, you should get a theory book and check it out (try *Theory for the Contemporary Guitarist*, by Guy Capuzzo or *The Complete Jazz Guitar Method* by Jody Fisher, both from the National Guitar Workshop and Alfred).

Johnny B. Blues Thing Transcription

Transcribed by Connor McCarthy

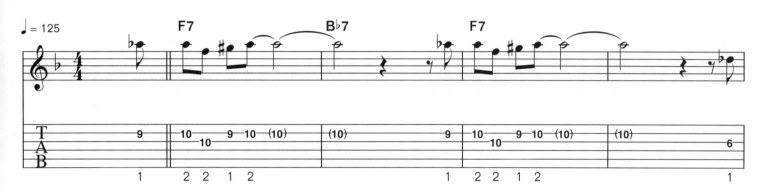

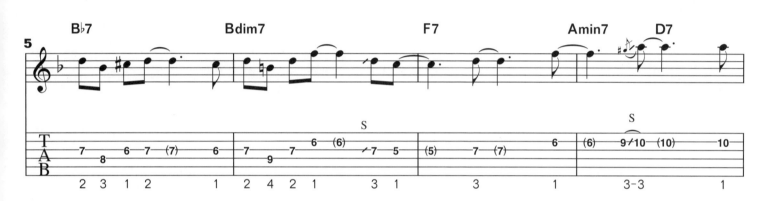

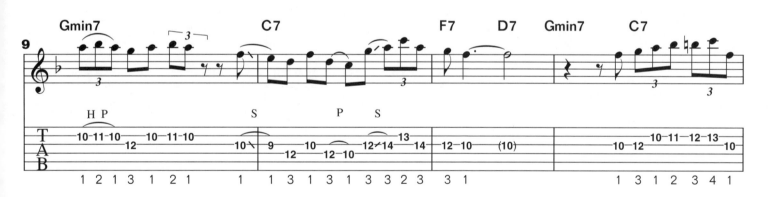

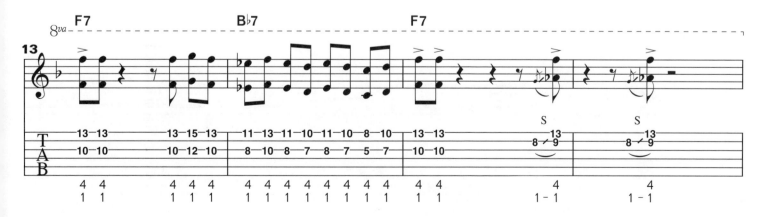

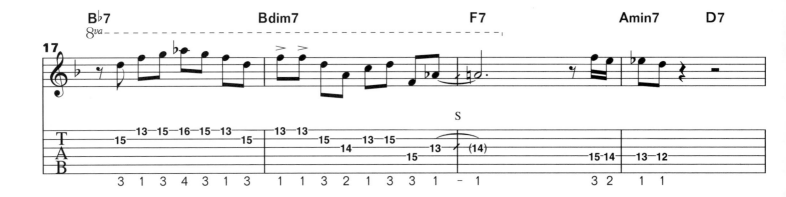

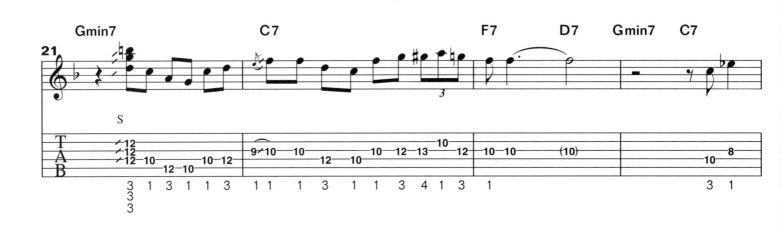

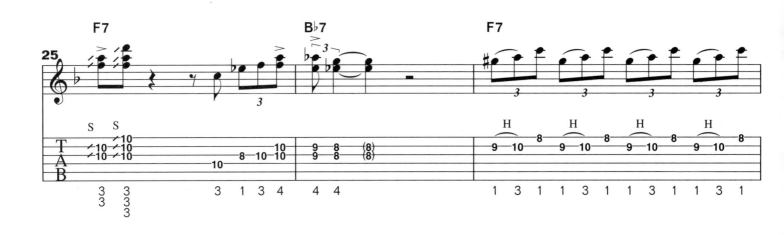

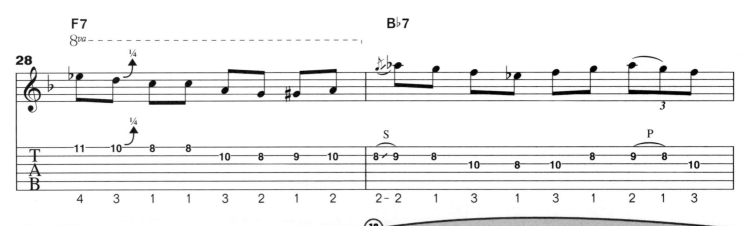

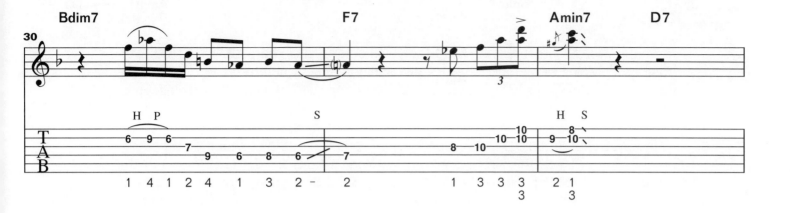

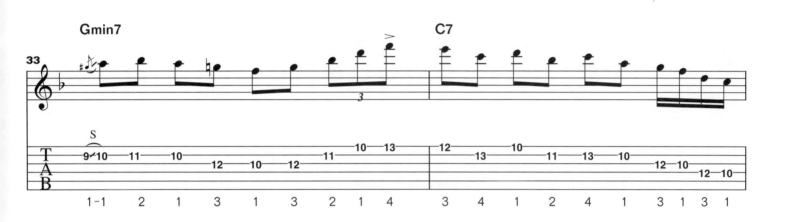

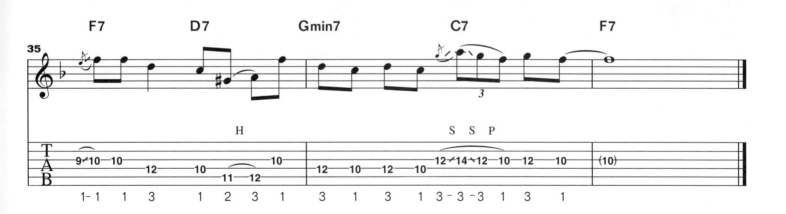

From the Wes Montgomery–style F Mixolydian octave lick in **bars 13–15**, to the 10th-position F Major Pentatonic and the major blues scales scattered throughout the solo, "Johnny B. Blues Thing" uses some staple jazz guitar devices that are essential knowledge.

In the first chorus, **bars 1–4** use the cool 7th-position F Major Blues scale shown below. You will see this scale again in the line in **bars 27–29** (starting with the eighth-note triplets). Note the added E♭ in **bar 28**. It gives the line a bluesy Mixolydian sound that continues into the B♭7 in a horizontal approach to playing over this chord change.

F Major Blues Scale

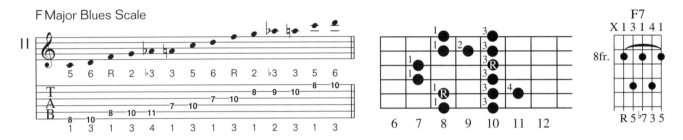

In **bar 5** you will see the B♭ Major Blues scale shown below. Also shown below is the Bdim7 arpeggio used in **bar 6** and **bar 30**. Notice how comfortable it feels to go from the B♭ Major Blues scale to the Bdim7 arpeggio. It is important to have good, flowing fingerings such as these when approaching improvisation vertically.

B♭ Major Blues Scale

Bdim7 Arpeggio

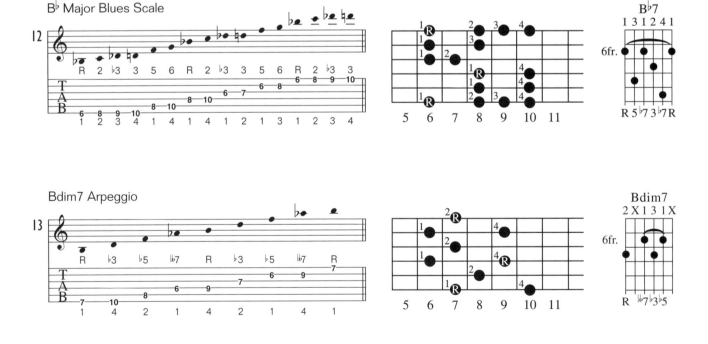

After the catchy ascending melody that starts on beat 4 of **bar 6** and climaxes in **bar 8**, you will find the 10th-position, one-octave G Dorian mode fingering covering the Gmin7 in **bar 9**. The fingering shown below starts on the ♭7 (F). Also, check out how this scale sneaks back in at **bar 12** for the ii–V in F, then again in **bar 33** and in the first two beats of **bar 34** for the Gmin7 and C7.

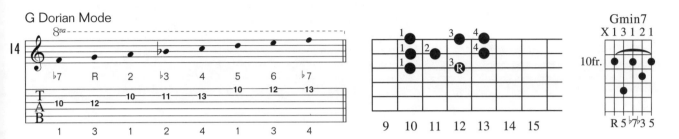

Even though the downbeat of **bar 10** is an E, which reinforces the C7 chord it's played over, the remainder of this line is all about the F Major Pentatonic scale shown below. Also, look for it in **bars 21–23** in a horizontal approach to playing over the ii–V in F, then (with some similarities to the line in bar 10) again in **bar 34**, beats 3 and 4 up to **bar 36**, to bring it on home. This scale is must-know!

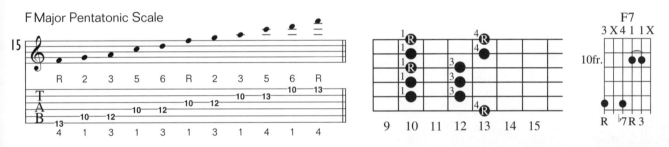

Charlie Parker (1920–1955) was arguably the greatest jazz saxophonist of all time. Slowing down his remarkably fast lines to half speed always reveals that every note made sense. "Bird," along with his contemporaries Dizzy Gillespie and Bud Powell, is considered one of the founders of bebop.

In bar 17, you will see another one-octave scale fingering starting on the ♭7. This one is the B♭ Mixolydian mode shown below. The line continues into **bar 18** with the F Major blues scale below.

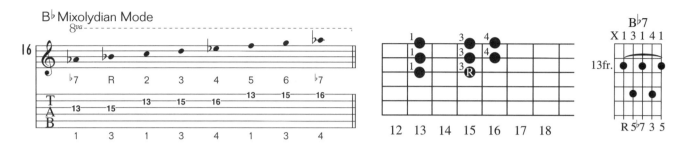

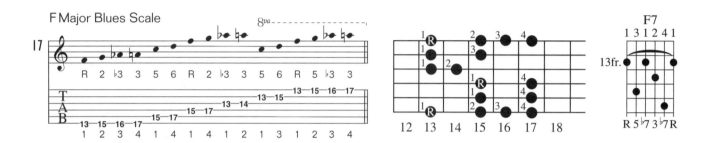

Thelonious Monk (1917–1982) was ignored for a decade before he was suddenly acclaimed as a genius. His music had not changed one bit in the meantime and was actually fully formed by 1947. He saw no need to alter his compositional style or piano playing during the next 25 years.

The Shower Test

Playing jazz requires guitarists to be at their most musical—right then and there on the bandstand. Jazz is creativity in motion, spontaneous composition, music of the moment. Above all, you need to practice being musical.

One surefire way to see if you are being musical is to take the Shower Test. The Shower Test is easy and it never lies. All you have to do is record yourself playing over the changes to any one of the charts in this book. Then, put the music aside and practice something else. During the next day or so, listen very closely to what you played, then hop in the shower and watch for the results. If you find yourself singing any of the lines from your solo in the shower, you have passed the test—even if it's just one.

If this seems hard to believe, or just plain stupid, then sit down and listen to *any* Miles Davis solo and see what happens. Try the solo from "Freddie the Freeloader" on the *Kind of Blue* CD. You will have to force yourself to stop singing his lines, even long after you first hear them (even when you're not in the shower).

All kidding aside, this is the real deal. If your lines are musical enough, simple or complex, they will stick in your head. If you are like many musicians, you are your toughest critic; so if *you* like it, so will everyone else!

*To study the career of **Miles Davis** (1926–1991) is to examine the history of jazz from the mid 1940s to the early '90s, as he was in the thick of almost every important innovation and stylistic development during that period, often leading the way.*

PHOTO • INSTITUTE OF JAZZ STUDIES

Solo 3

The Chart

"Autumn Breeze" is a three-chorus, 32-bar **AABC** tune in the style of the mega-standard "Autumn Leaves." The letters **AABC** tell us that there are three different sections—**A**, **B** and **C**—and that the first of them is repeated before going on to the next two, **B** and **C**. Both jazz and classical musicians use this method of discussing *form* (the way a piece of music is organized).

This set of changes is an easy introduction to soloing over obvious shifts in key center and provides your first chance to solo in a non-blues format. *Autumn Leaves* can be found on loads of recordings by master soloists, which gives a beginning improviser many sources from which to draw inspiration.

Here are the changes:

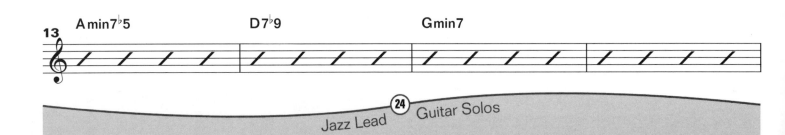

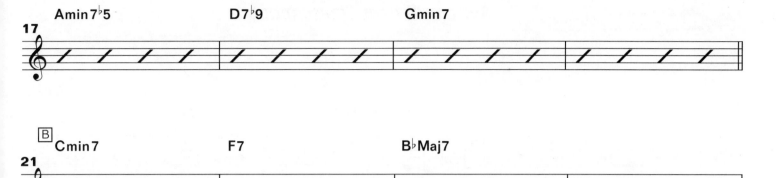

- The two **A** sections and the **B** section *modulate* (change key) between B♭ Major and G Minor, which are *relative* major and minor keys (they share the same key signature). This allows you to use a horizontal approach, as in the solo played on the CD and transcribed on the following pages.

- Listen to the tritone substitutions in the ii–Vs in **bars 27 and 28** of the **C** section. The G♭7 and E7 create *chromatic* (half-step) bass movement in the ii–Vs leading to the E♭Maj7 in **bar 29**: G–G♭–F–E– E♭. To further clarify what is happening, think of it this way:

    The G♭7 is a tritone sub for C7, V7 of the Fmin7 chord it precedes. Instead of Gmin7–C7–Fmin7 (ii–V7–i), we get Gmin7–G♭7–Fmin7.

    The E7 is a tritone sub for B♭7, V7 of the E♭Maj7 chord it precedes. Instead of Fmin7–B♭7–E♭Maj7 (ii–V7–I), we get Fmin7–E7–E♭Maj7.

This is a very hip sound to solo over, and can be heard in almost any style. These changes can be approached both horizontally and vertically.

- Check out how the rhythm section kicks in at the third chorus to give the solo a dynamic twist. The drummer moves from a hi-hat pulse on beats 2 and 4 (this is called a *backbeat* feel) to a four-beat feel on the ride cymbal. The bass line also shifts from a two-beat feel to an aggressive yet smooth four-beat feel, creating a more driving momentum in the overall vibe.

With Solo, Track 6
Backing Track, Track 7

Autumn Breeze Transcription

Transcribed by Connor McCarthy

♩ = 176

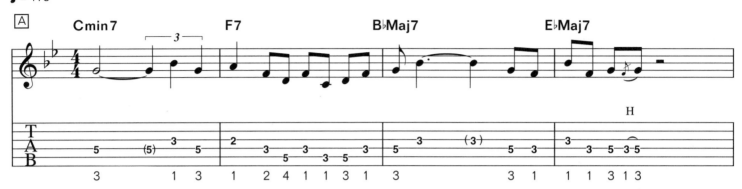

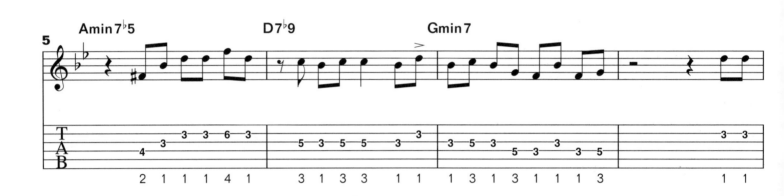

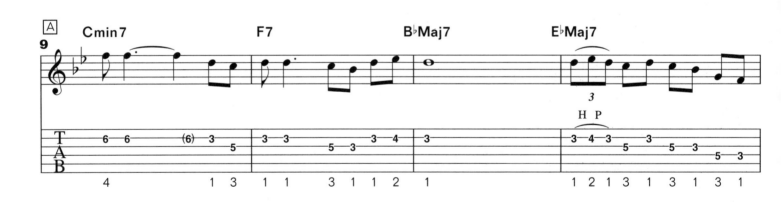

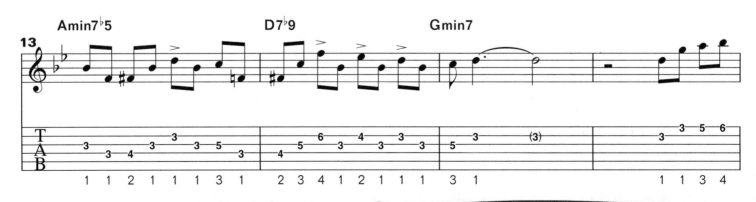

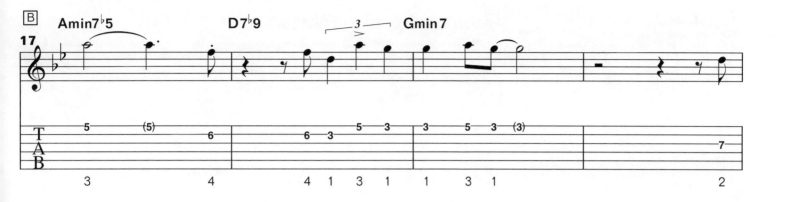

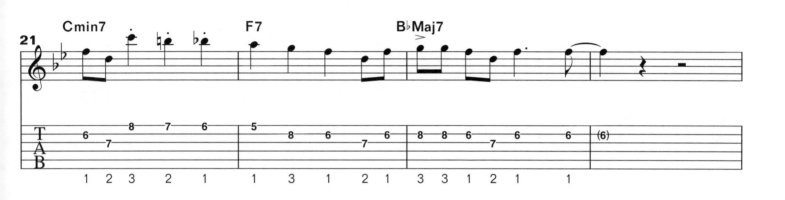

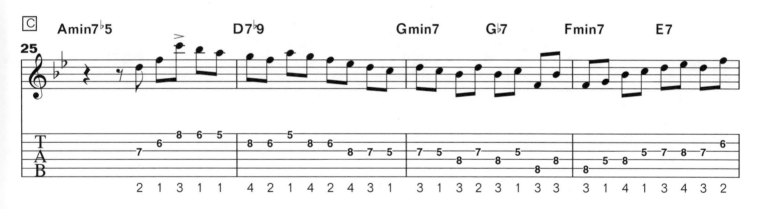

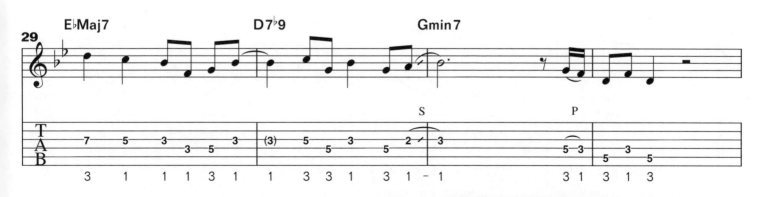

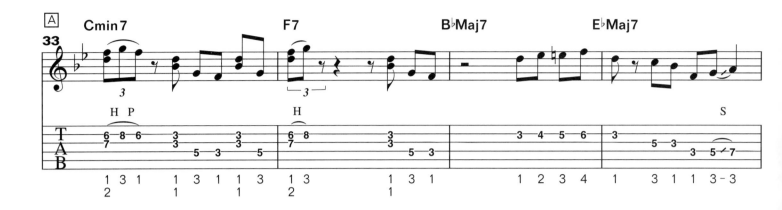

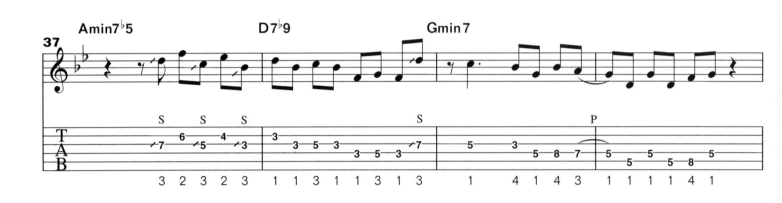

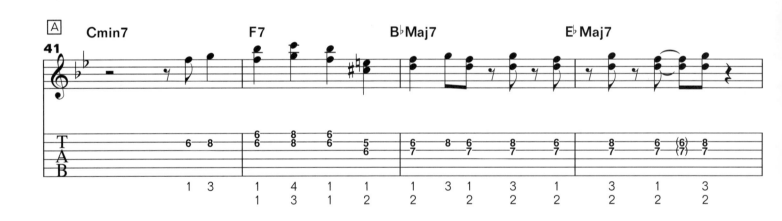

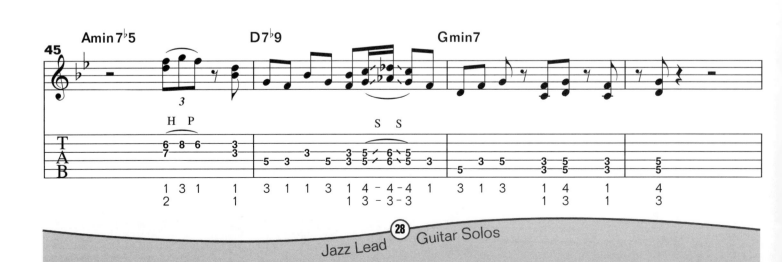

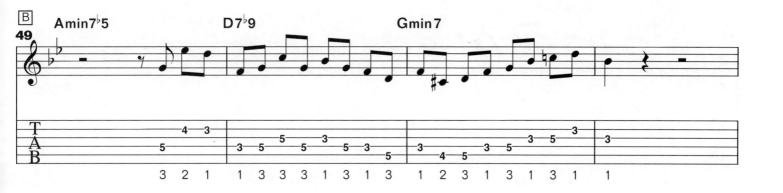

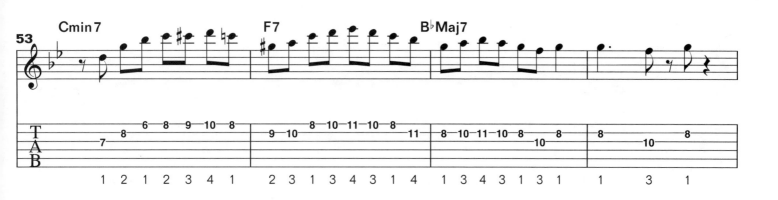

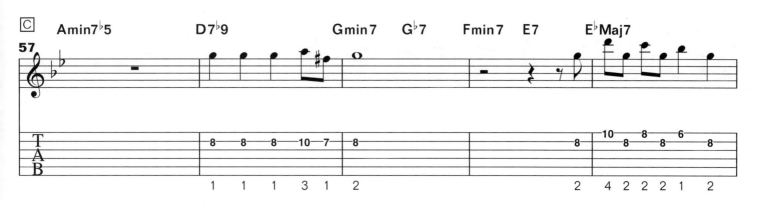

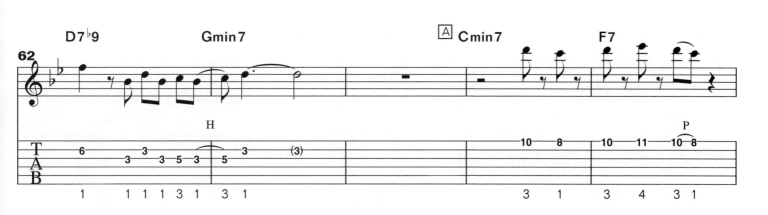

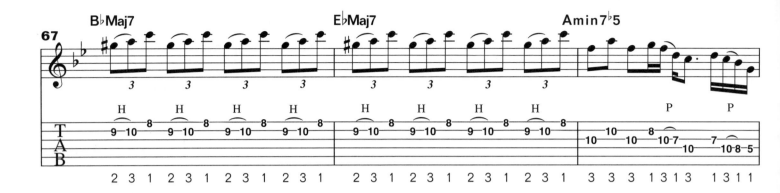

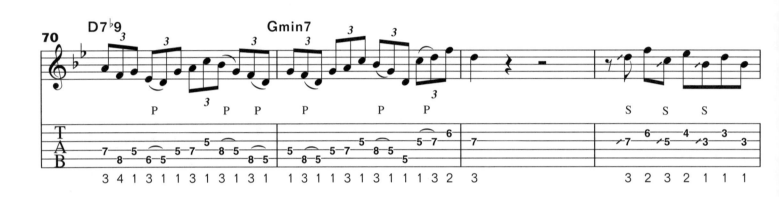

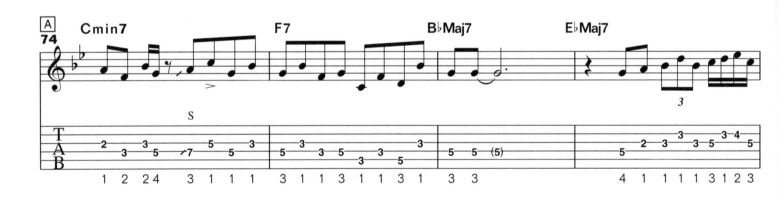

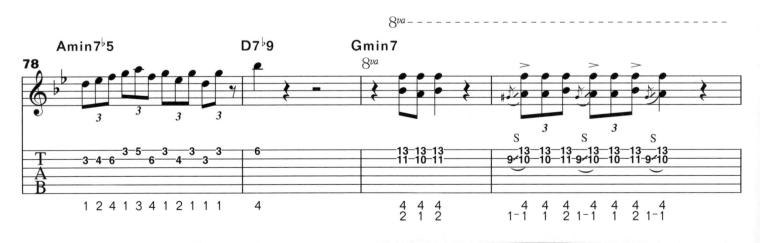

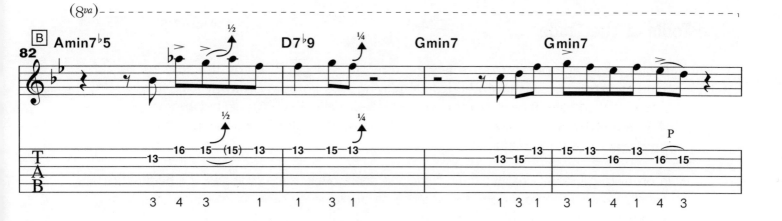

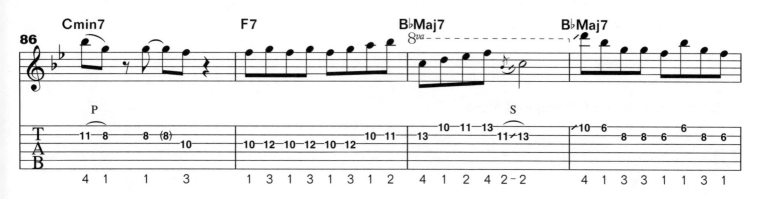

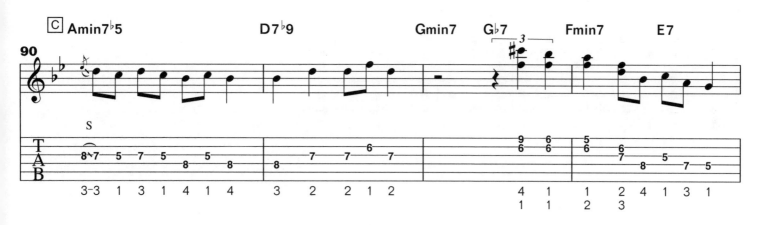

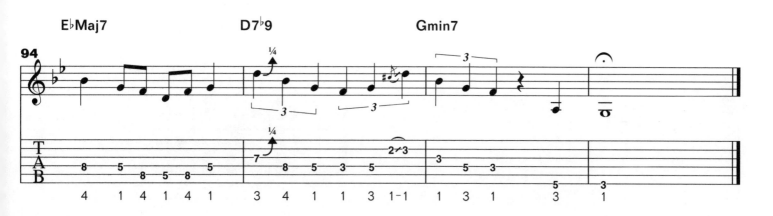

Taking advantage of the relative key centers of B♭ Major/G Minor, the solo in "Autumn Breeze" is focused on horizontal playing; the notes are drawn almost exclusively from one set of seven diatonic notes (B♭–C–D–E♭–F–G–A). Or, put another way, only one scale is used, but the root shifts between B♭ and G. Put simply, this is an easy way for you to sound hip.

In order to generate creative lines from one scale over these changes, it's helpful to visualize the fretboard as one extended area of diatonic notes. Below is a "diatonic roadmap" from which the solo was played. Clearly visualizing one large, extended scale over the fretboard frees you from being "locked" into positional (box-pattern) fingerings, which can limit your note choices and phrasing. It enables *you* to play the guitar, rather than having the *guitar* play you.

Pay close attention to the uppercase **R** for major roots and the lowercase **r** for minor roots.

Diatonic Roadmap of B♭ Major/G Minor

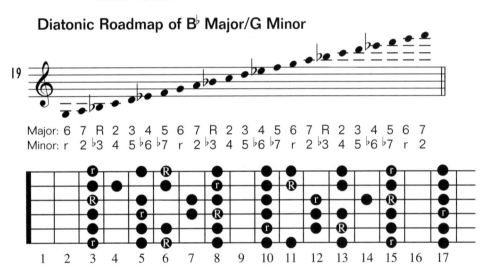

R = Root of B♭ Major
r = Root of G Minor

Here's the roadmap broken down into seven logical one-position fingerings that start and end on each successive scale tone (the first one starts on G, the second on A, and so on). Notice that they all overlap. Again, remember that an uppercase **R** is for a major root and a lowercase **r** is for a minor root.

Fingering 1: Starting on G

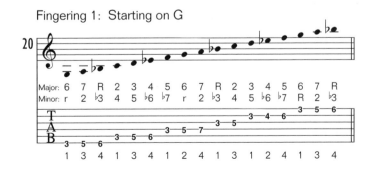

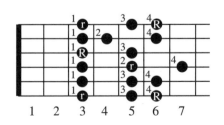

Fingering 2: Starting on A

21

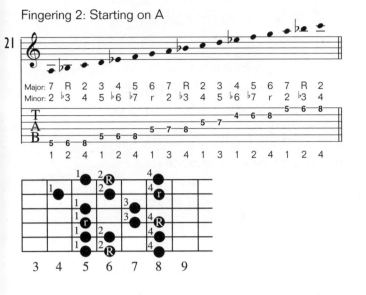

Major:	7	R	2	3	4	5	6	7	R	2	3	4	5	6	7	R	2
Minor:	2	♭3	4	5	♭6	♭7	r	2	♭3	4	5	♭6	♭7	r	2	♭3	4

Fingering 3: Starting on B♭

22

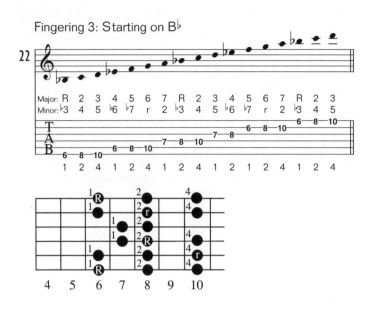

Major:	R	2	3	4	5	6	7	R	2	3	4	5	6	7	R	2	3
Minor:	♭3	4	5	♭6	♭7	r	2	♭3	4	5	♭6	♭7	r	2	♭3	4	5

Fingering 4: Starting on C

23

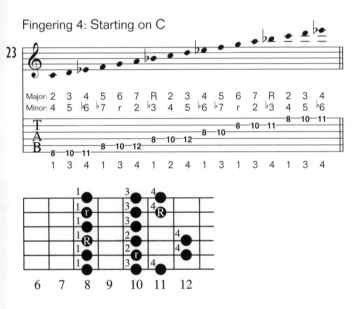

Major:	2	3	4	5	6	7	R	2	3	4	5	6	7	R	2	3	4
Minor:	4	5	♭6	♭7	r	2	♭3	4	5	♭6	♭7	r	2	♭3	4	5	♭6

Fingering 5: Starting on D

24

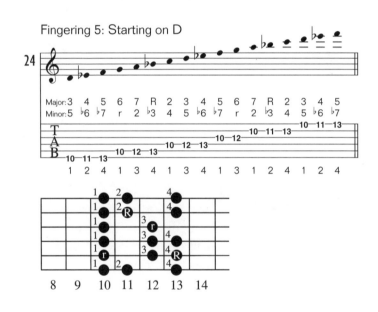

Major:	3	4	5	6	7	R	2	3	4	5	6	7	R	2	3	4	5
Minor:	5	♭6	♭7	r	2	♭3	4	5	♭6	♭7	r	2	♭3	4	5	♭6	♭7

Fingering 6: Starting on E♭

25

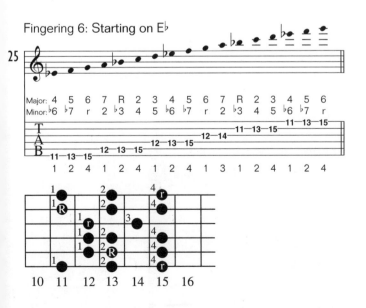

Major:	4	5	6	7	R	2	3	4	5	6	7	R	2	3	4	5	6
Minor:	♭6	♭7	r	2	♭3	4	5	♭6	♭7	r	2	♭3	4	5	♭6	♭7	r

Fingering 7: Starting on F

26

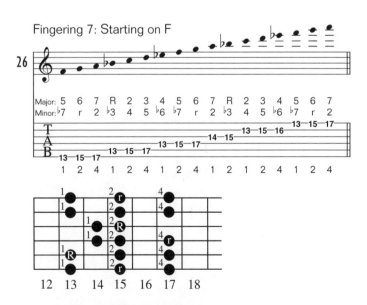

Major:	5	6	7	R	2	3	4	5	6	7	R	2	3	4	5	6	7
Minor:	♭7	r	2	♭3	4	5	♭6	♭7	r	2	♭3	4	5	♭6	♭7	r	2

Playing the Roadmap

There are no matching chord shapes in this chapter because the lines were not played with specific shapes and arpeggios in mind. They were played in a horizontal approach, with more attention to melodic content.

First Chorus

With the exception of the occasional F♯ in both minor ii–Vs (**bars 5–6 and 13–14**), and a B♮ in **bar 21** of the B section, the entire first chorus is played from B♭ Major and G Minor diatonic melodies. The B♮ is a *chromatic passing tone*, which is simply a non-chord tone connecting two chord tones by half step. The F♯ is a little more significant. The F♯ is a half step below the root of the Gmin7 you are approaching, and the tension it creates strongly pulls the melodies towards it. Tension, as you will hear and see throughout this book and beyond, needs resolution. We start building that tension as early as the Amin7♭5 chord, which results in a greater feeling of release or resolution at the Gmin7.

Fingerings 1 and 2 will work well for playing the lines in the first chorus. If you analyze the note content in the lines, you will see that even though we are using a horizontal approach, there are plenty of chord tones. As you improvise, let your ear be your guide so you can develop a natural sense of melody that matches the changes. This will help your lines sound more *real*, because you're playing for the music and not the fingering.

Second Chorus

The second chorus begins with the same scale fingerings as the first chorus and uses similar melodic ideas. In **bar 54–59**, there's a shift to Fingering 4, while **bars 60, 61,** and the first beat of **bar 62** use Fingering 3. The chorus ends at **bars 62 and 63** with a small melody out of Fingering 1 before going into the third and final chorus.

Third chorus

In the third chorus, you will hear a change in the overall attitude of the solo due to the rhythm section's shift from a two-beat feel to a stronger four-beat feel. As a result, you will hear and see more motion in the solo move to go along with the rise in the band's intensity.

The third chorus begins with Fingering 4 at **bar 65** but quickly shifts into the triplet lick in **bars 67 and 68** (in the style of Grant Green). That run continues down into Fingering 3 in **bar 69** and then Fingering 2 for **bars 71 and 72**. **Bars 73–79** start out in Fingering 2 and continue into Fingering 1.

For the George Benson–style double-stop lick in **bars 80 and 81**, make sure you hold down the left-hand 4th finger on the 1st string, 13th fret (F), while the 1st and 2nd fingers glide through the 2nd-string chromatic sequence. **Bars 82–85** are played with Fingering 7. **Bars 87 and 88** move briefly into Fingering 5, then begin a descending run from Fingering 4 in **bar 89** down to Fingering 1 to the end.

Now try to come up with your own lines over these changes and remember to always listen to the music around you and not just your solo; use the music around you to inspire the music inside you.

Feel

The importance of how you interpret the *feel* of jazz could be the single most important concept for you to grasp. Your feel is the most basic component to your musicianship and will be a big part of your identity as an improviser. It is also among the most difficult ideas to explain, but here goes….

Sometimes it's not about *what* note you play as much as it's about *where* you put it. One note, thoughtfully placed in just the right spot, can bring the house down.

You can practice feel by listening to music. Listen for how your favorite players spontaneously create the music you love. Listen to how the notes flow from one to another, how an improviser reacts to the band and how the band reacts to him or her. Listen not only to instrumentalists, but to vocalists as well. Try to find multiple versions of the same tune and carefully take notice of the approach taken by each group and individual player. Listen to it long enough so that you can sing your favorite solo from memory. That's *feelin'* it!

To better understand what to listen for, listen very closely to the "Autumn Breeze" solo on the CD (track 6) and concentrate on the concepts listed below:

Swing

Playing swing 8ths (see page 7) is the first and foremost element of playing with a jazz feel. Count triplet eighth notes aloud against the pulse, saying "1–2–3, 1–2–3," and so on. If you have trouble finding the triplet groove, check out the opening line of the third chorus (bar 67) for a definitive example of triplets. Once you have the flow, drop the "2" out of your count, say the "3" with a little more meaning and you'll have a good idea what swing feel is supposed to sound like.

Accents

Playing a note with a little more emphasis than the others around it creates an *accent*. Accents can profoundly change the way your line feels. For example, listen to **bars 12–15**, and pay attention to the way some notes almost jump out and make the line dance.

Space

Space gives jazz its groove and its overall coolness. This solo is packed with air. Just listen to all the spots where you hear the beautiful sound of nothing. A great way to introduce space into your playing is to take a deep breath before you play a line, exhale as you play it, and when your breath's all gone … stop playing! Even if you're not done with your idea, stop. This will not only help you play with space, but will help you organize your lines into concise ideas that will have far more impact. You will hear an immediate difference in your solos when you incorporate this important tool into your playing.

These concepts will be present throughout every solo in this book.

Solo 4

The Chart

"Rodney's Groove" is a one-chorus **ABC** chart in a funky, smooth-jazz style with some hints of disco. This E Dorian jam is in the style of the José Feliciano tune "Affirmation," which was recorded by George Benson. Following the approach of the more straight-ahead "Autumn Breeze," this chart can also be soloed over with a mostly horizontal approach, but with some funky phrasing.

Here's the chord progression:

Straight 8ths

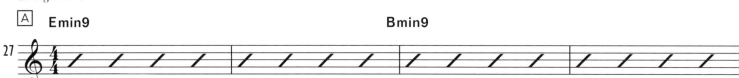

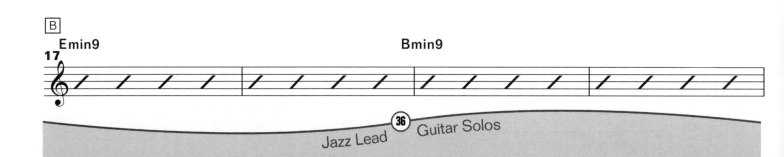

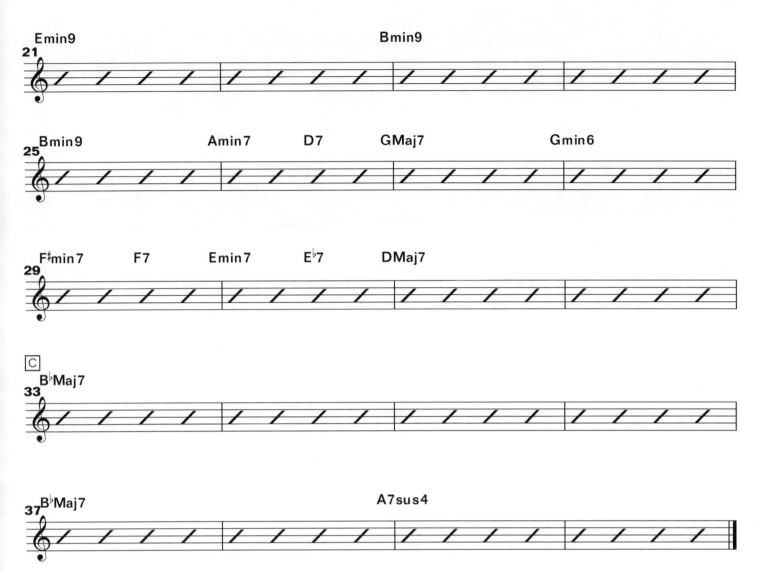

- As in "Autumn Breeze," in **bars 29 and 30** you will hear chromatic bass movement in the ii–Vs as a result of the tritone substitutions (see page 25). Another way of describing this kind of series of ii–Vs is with the term *back cycling*. Back cycling is essentially working backward from a desired destination. In this case, the destination is DMaj7. We get there through a short series of two ii–V–I progressions (with tritone substitutions for the Vs). The resolution of the first ii–V becomes the ii of the next ii–V. If these or any set of changes within a chart give you a problem, isolate them and practice soloing over those changes exclusively until they become comfortable.

- Listen to how the tasty B♭Maj7 in **bars 33 to 38** adds a welcome piece of ear candy for you to solo over. This is the first modulation in this book that takes us outside the realm of a relative key.

- Notice how the rhythm section stays in a tight, precise groove behind the solo. This allows the soloist to stretch out rhythmically as well as melodically.

Rodney's Groove Transcription

Transcribed by Doug Osborn

♩ = 108

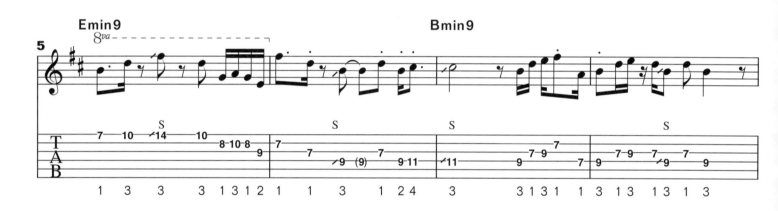

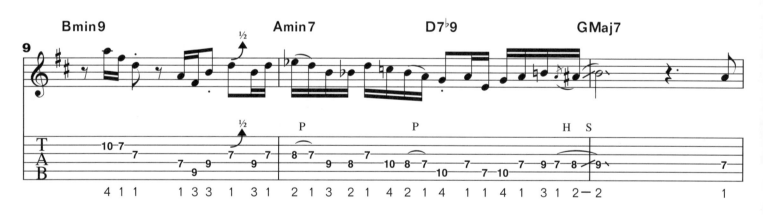

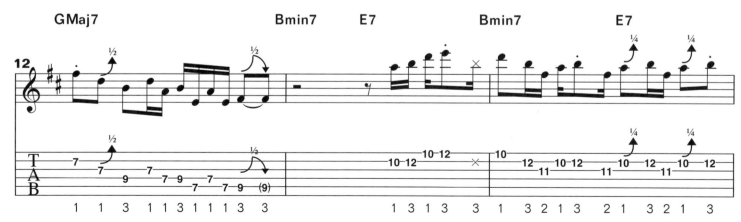

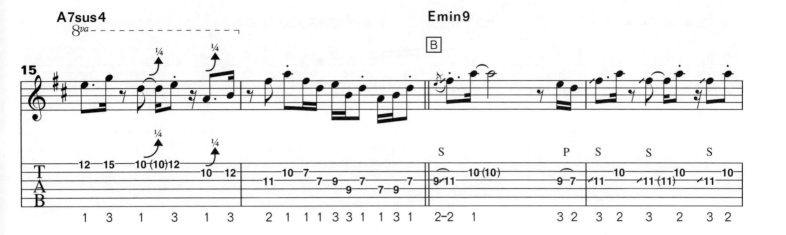

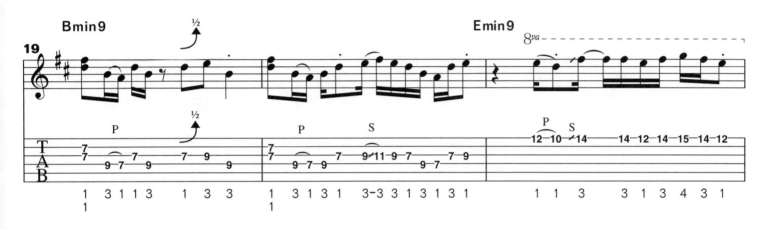

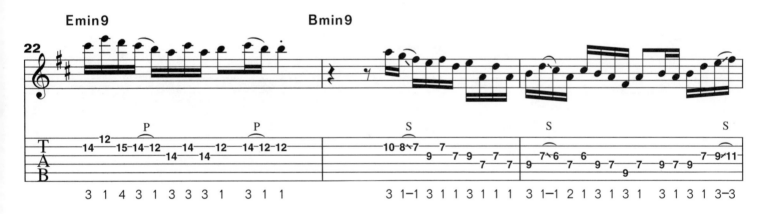

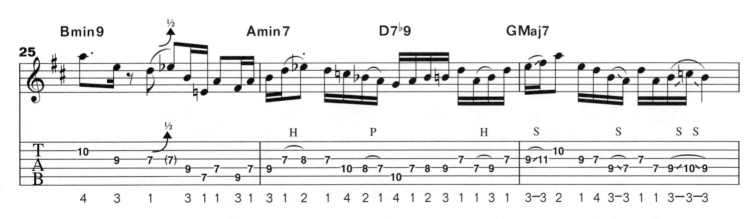

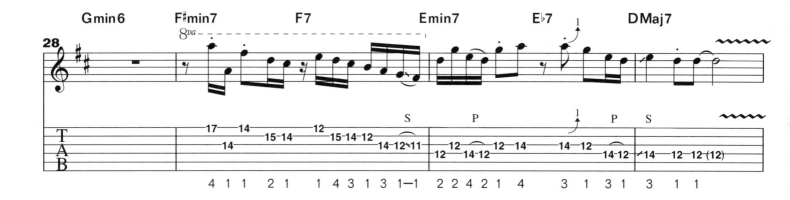

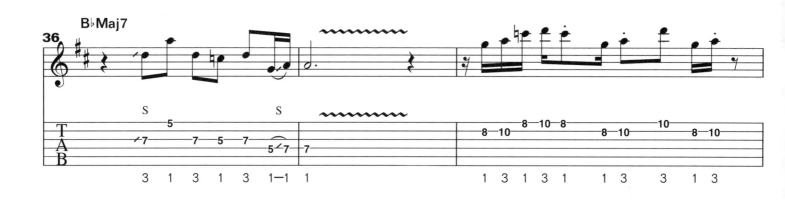

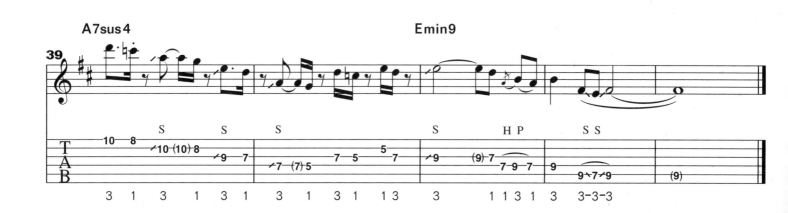

Like "Autumn Breeze," "Rodney's Groove" has a great deal of horizontal playing because the harmony allows it. Also like "Autumn Breeze," you will see that the horizontal lines were not left to just one scale. What's different in this case is that more of the horizontal lines were played with chord shapes and chord tones in mind, and there were some passages played with a vertical approach. The matching chord shapes, therefore, will appear in the following discussion when appropriate.

With the exception of the high F♯ (the 9 of the Emin9 chord) on the 1st string, 14th fret, in **bar 5**, the solo starts out in the 7th-position B Aeolian mode shown below. This scale produces the horizontal lines for **bars 1–9** and **bars 23–24**.

B Aeolian Mode

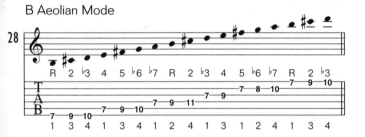
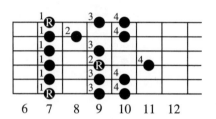

Here comes some of the fun stuff. For the two-beat ii–V in the key of G Major in **bars 10 and 26**, the D Mixolydian ♭9 scale shown below delivers an effective altered sound without getting too out.

D Mixolydian ♭9 Mode

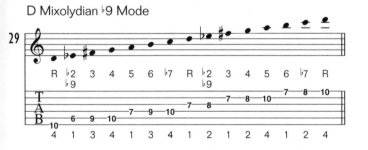
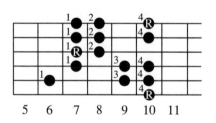

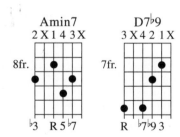

The 7th-position B Minor Pentatonic scale fingering shown below was used for **bar 12** to play with a horizontal approach across the GMaj7 chord. It also covered the A7sus4 in **bar 16**, all of the lines in **bars 17–20**, and the Bmin9 in **bar 25**.

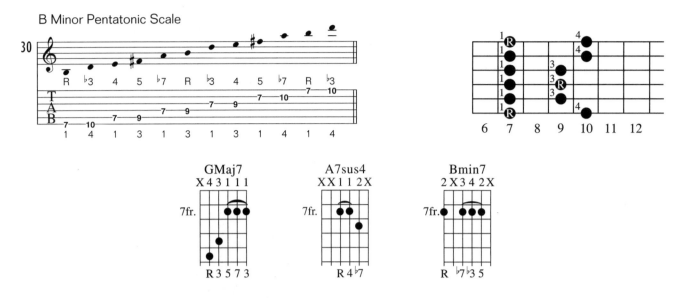

In **bars 13 and 14**, you will hear the 9th-position B Minor Pentatonic fingering shown below continue the horizontal run. This time it's over the two-beat ii–V in the key of A Major. It was also used to cover the A7sus4 in **bar 15** with the addition of the 1st-string, 15th-fret G (the ♭7 of the chord).

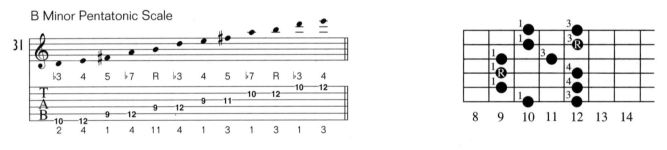

This 14th-position B Aeolian fingering was used for the horizontal lines in **bars 21 and 22**.

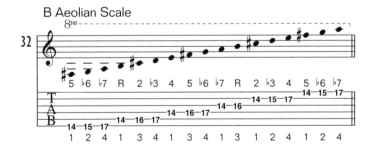
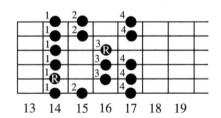

Jazz Lead Guitar Solos

For the back-cycling ii–Vs in **bars 29 and 30**, this D Major arpeggio and D Major scale were used to stream across the changes to resolve nicely on the DMaj7.

DMaj7 Arpeggio

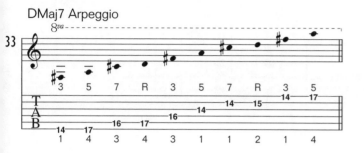

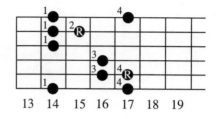

D Major Scale

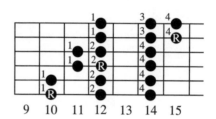

The B♭ Major (G Minor) scale initally shown on page 32 starts the line leading into the catchy B♭Maj7 chord in **bar 33**. It begins in the 6th position and migrates down to 5th position.

B♭ Major/G Minor Scale

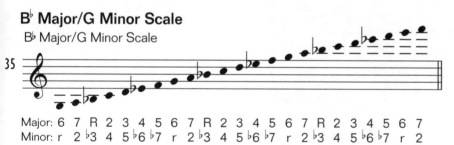

R = Root of B♭ Major
r = Root of G Minor

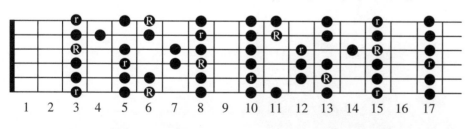

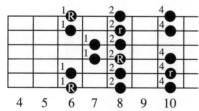

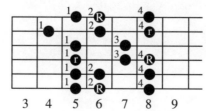

The two A Minor Pentatonic scales below are used for a horizontal approach to the rest of the solo in **bars 35–40** until the final Emin9 is hit in **bar 41**. Superimposing these A Minor Pentatonic scales over the B♭Maj7 allows you to play the major 7th (A), major 2nd or 9th (C) major 3rd (D), ♯4th or ♯11th (E) and major 6th or 13th (G) over the chord.

A Minor Pentatonic Scale: 5th Position

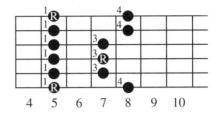

A Minor Pentatonic Scale: 7th Position

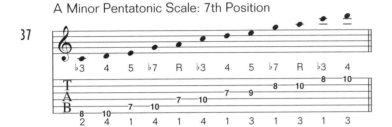
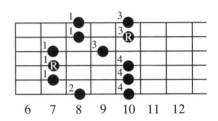

Herbie Hancock (born in 1940), is one of the most revered and controversial figures in jazz. With deep roots in the work of his mentor Mies Davis and other legendary artists such as Bill Evans, he has also crossed over into the smooth jazz field.

That's the Fact, Jack!

Following are some cold, hard facts about what a great jazz solo should have.

A Story to Tell

A basic yet important aspect of a good jazz solo is the form. You have to tell a story, so it must have a beginning, middle and an end. Start out slowly, build the plot, and then end it with a dive-bomb Steve Vai would be proud of. Okay, maybe a dive-bomb isn't the way to go for a jazz solo, but you get the idea—you need a climax.

Use Space

Another essential aspect of a good jazz solo is the use of *space* (time when you don't play, see the discussion on page 35).

Leading In

A key component to developing a good jazz feel in your solos is to learn the concept of leading in. *Leading in*, *pulling in*, or *playing ahead* is beginning your line for a given chord before the actual chord arrives. This gives your solo forward motion, and without that, your solos will sound stiff and clumsy. Also, this gives an indication as to where you're going with the line, further enhancing your communication with the band, which is very important.

Summary

Leading in will help while you are working on improving your use of space in the organization of complete solos. When you get these techniques into your playing, it's almost impossible to imagine one without the other.

Be sure to listen for these concepts in action during all of the solos in this book and CD.

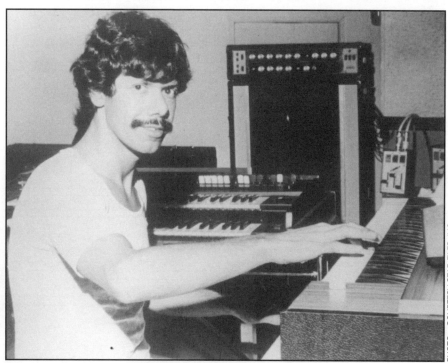

*Born in 1941, **Chick Corea** was one of the top pianists to emerge after Bill Evans and McCoy Tyner. He is also one of the few electric keyboardists to be quite individual and recognizable on synthesizers. Corea has composed several jazz standards, including "Spain," "La Fiesta," and "Windows."*

Solo 5

The Chart

The Head

The *head* is the main melody of a tune. The head is also one of the main sources from which we draw ideas for a solo. "Flipper Lane" is the first piece in this book with a head, making it an actual tune (remember, that's jazz lingo for a "song").

As with most components of jazz, the head is open to interpretation. It's understood and encouraged that the musician who plays the head will stamp his or her own individual character on it through rhythmic variations or melodic embellishments.

The tunes in this book will be written in a format you may see in jazz fake books or even charts from composers. Notice that the standard music notation of the head is written down an octave. This is the way all the heads in this book will appear. Usually, a guitarist will play the head an octave higher than written to make it stand out from the accompaniment.

Back to a more traditional straight-ahead feel, "Flipper Lane" is a 32-bar **ABAC** chart in C Major in the style of the popular standard "On Green Dolphin Street." The solo on this three-chorus tune has the head in the first chorus followed by a two-chorus improvisation. Its changes must be dealt with vertically due to the frequent shifts of key center. Keep the melody in mind and let it guide you. As with "Autumn Breeze," there's no shortage of excellent recordings of "On Green Dolphin Street" to listen to and study.

Here are the changes and the head.

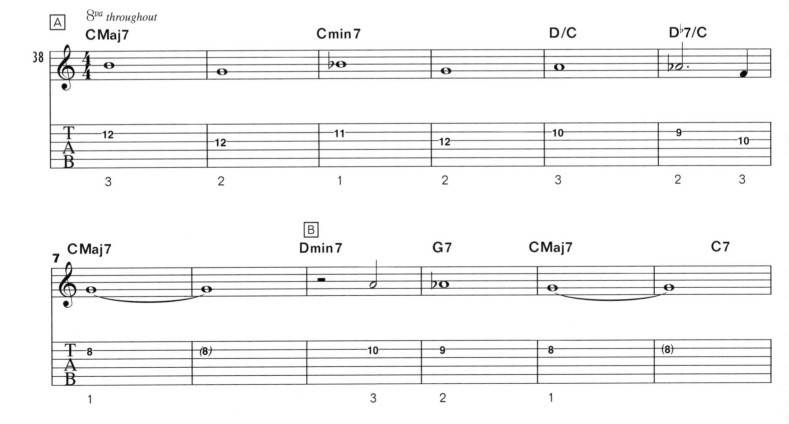

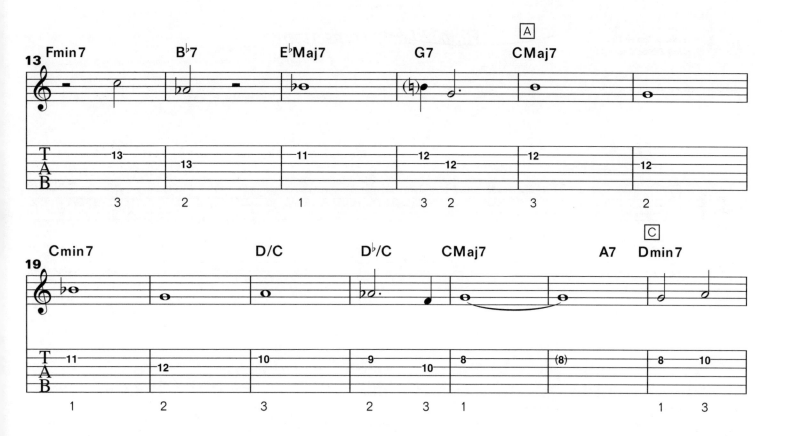

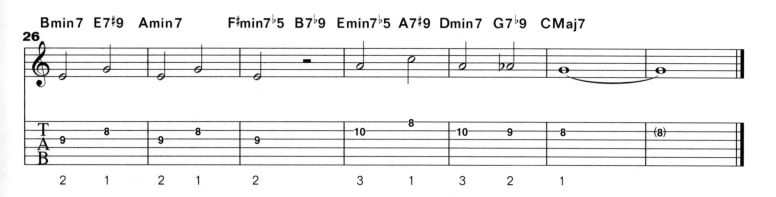

- Compared to the **B** and **C** sections, the **A** section sets a definitive mood to return to throughout the tune. Building ideas that fit the moods of contrasting sections enhances a solo.

- Starting in the **C** section at **bar 28**, the series of ii–Vs that eventually resolves to the CMaj7 is another good example of back cycling (see page 37). This is a standard practice in jazz harmony, so be sure to listen to the effect it creates. As you experiment with creating your own solos, try both horizontal and vertical approaches to these ii–Vs.

Enjoy!

Flipper Lane Transcription

Transcribed by Steve Hager

♩ = 163

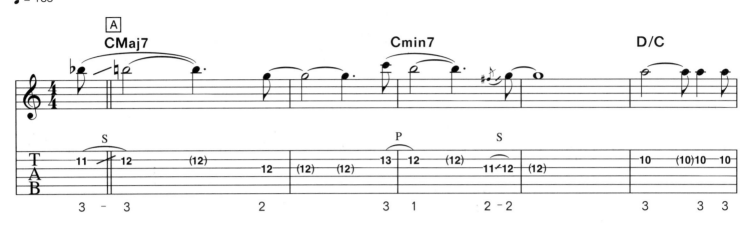

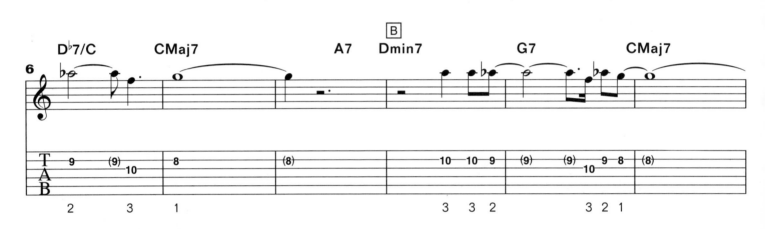

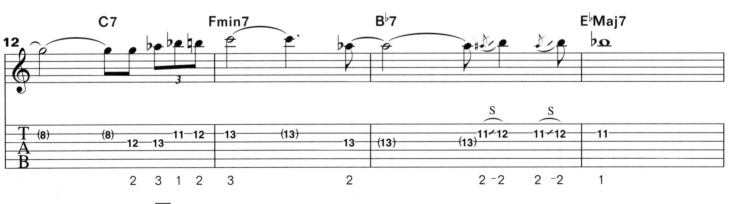

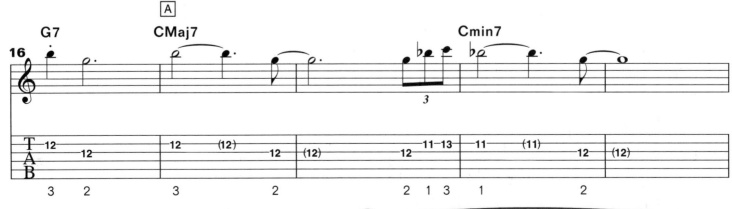

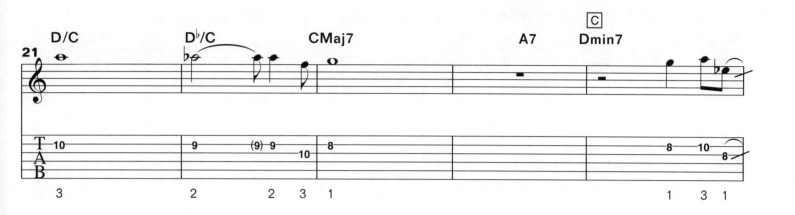

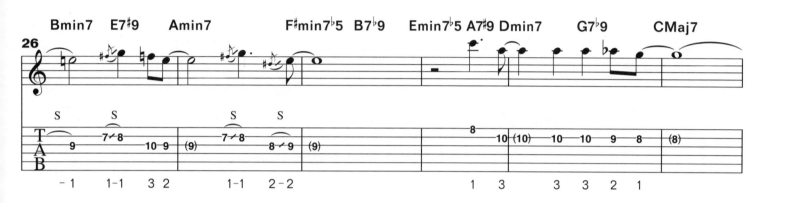

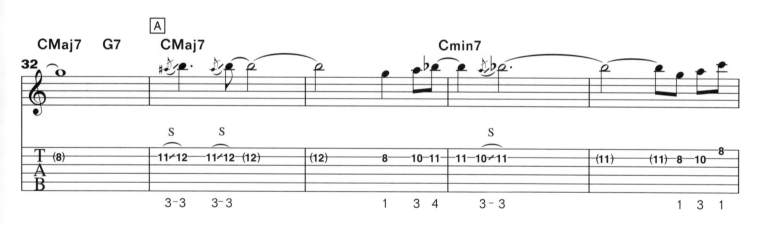

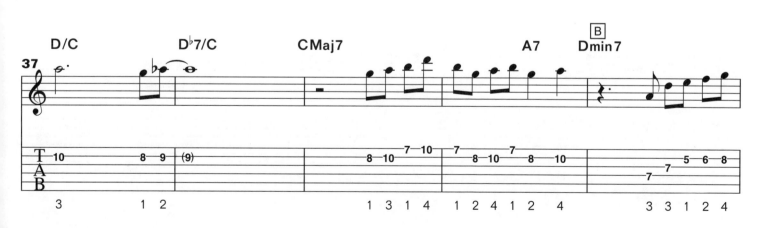

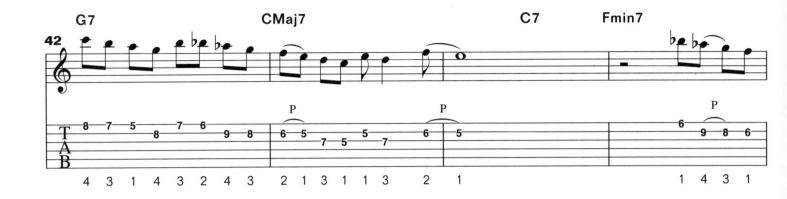

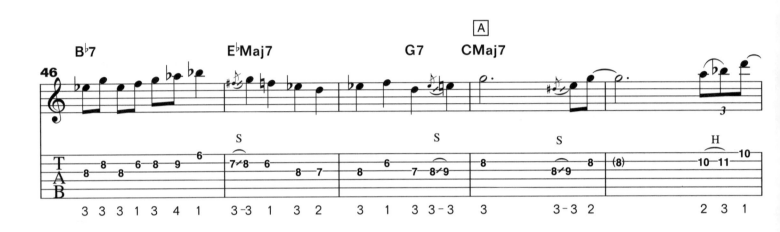

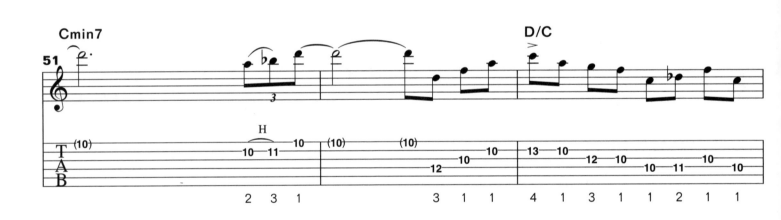

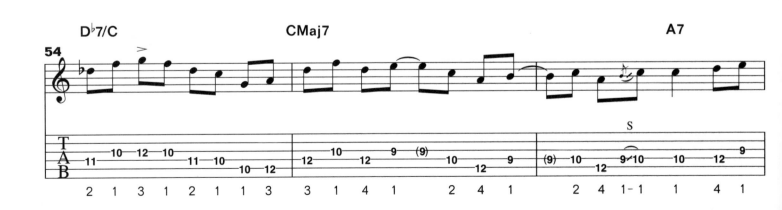

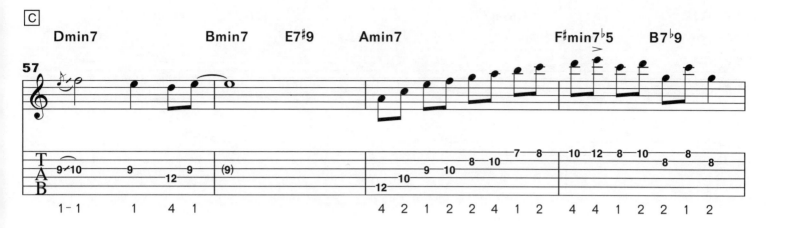

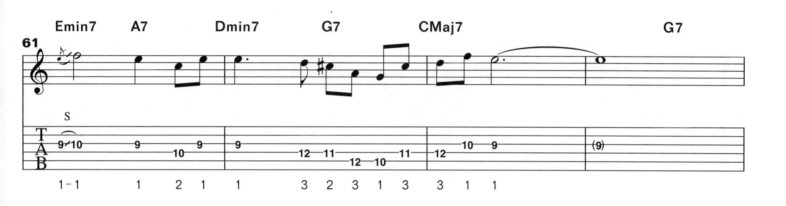

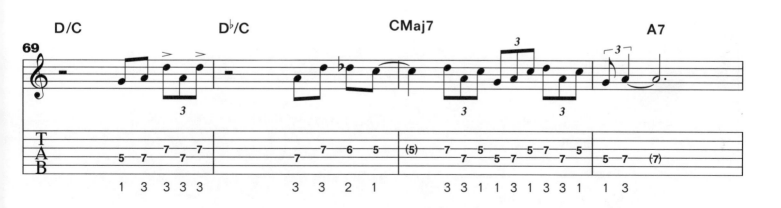

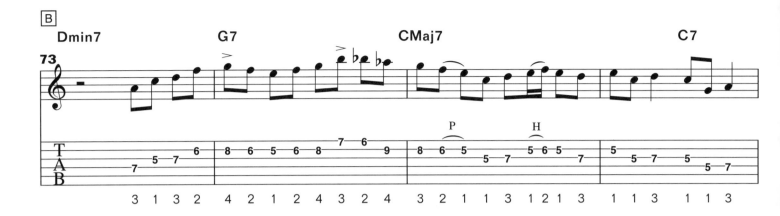

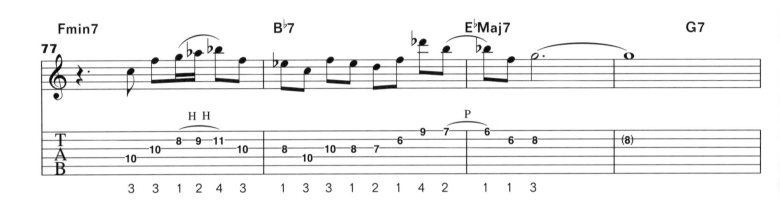

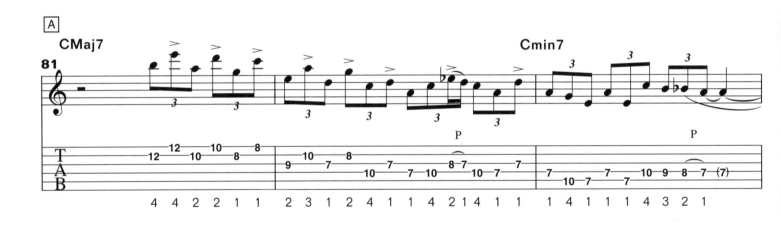

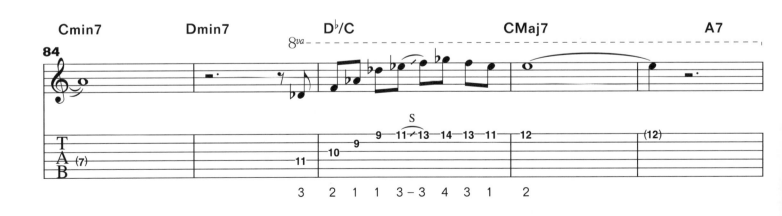

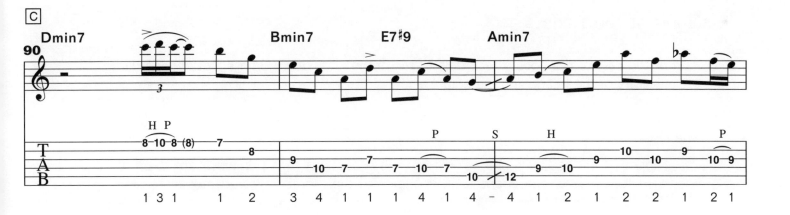

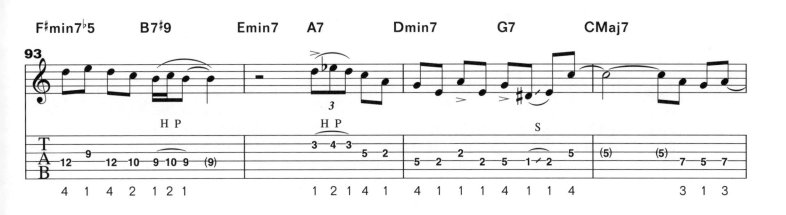

For the rest of the book, the "Tools of the Trade" lessons will be split between discussions of the heads and the solos.

The Head

"Flipper Lane" has a simple melody. For the **A** sections, it is primarily composed of chord tones. Even the **B** and **C** sections, with their more involved melodies, stay close to the chord tones.

Rhythmic Variation: Anticipation of the Downbeat

To keep any stiffness out of the melody, we can shift a note that is written on the *downbeat* (the first beat of a complete bar) to the preceding *upbeat* (the last half of the fourth beat).

Just look at the chart for of this solo and compare it to the transcription of the actual performance of the solo on the CD (be sure to do the same in the next three chapters as well). As you listen to the solo, you will hear the good effect of the anticipations. For example, the first two notes of the head are B and G. In the unembellished version of the head in the chart, the G comes on the downbeat of bar 2. In the solo, it comes on the last half of the upbeat to bar 2—the last half beat of bar 1. This is an excellent example of anticipation.

Embellishments: Adding or Subtracting Notes

Adding notes to the written melody is another tool for personalizing the head. Whether it is a slide from a half step below, a repetition of a note, or a walk-up with scale tones to the actual note, it's these little embellishments that make the written melody more musical.

Check out some these examples of embellishment in the solo's transcription:

Bar 1: The chromatic slide up to the first written note of the head.

Bar 5: The rhythmic repetition of the written whole note.

Bar 12: The walk-up to the written note in bar 13.

The Solo

Due to the frequent modulations in the more advanced solos in this book, the explanations will concentrate on the most important tools of the trade for playing over these more involved chord progressions.

From the opening of the improvised section of the solo in the **A** section **at bars 33–38**, you can hear the head clearly reiterated in the solo ideas. This is the most basic yet tasteful way to start your improvisation.

Moving on, we have a classic vertical ii–V lick in **bars 41–44** and **bars 73–76**. The D Dorian scale below is played over the Dmin7 chords, followed by the G Altered scale over the G7 chords. You should practice this lick, as well as all others you learn, in all keys.

D Dorian Scale

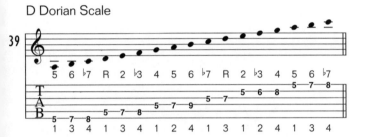
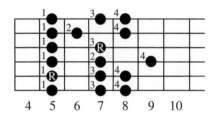

Dmin7
X 1 3 1 2 1

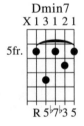

G Altered Scale

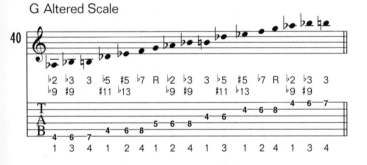
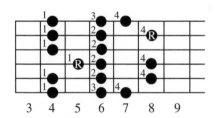

G7♭9
2 X 1 3 1 X

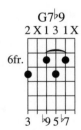

Check out the smooth vertical transition between the CMaj7 and Cmin7 chords in **bars 65–68**. The two scale fingerings below will work well for creating a line. When a chord changes to another chord with the same root, it's known as a *parallel change* or *mutation*. Parallel changes are an easy way to get comfortable with soloing with a vertical approach.

C Major Scale—10th Position

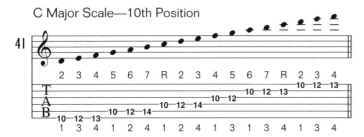

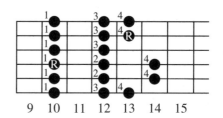

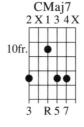

C Dorian Mode

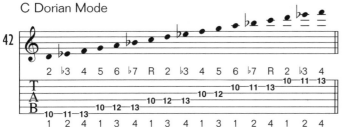

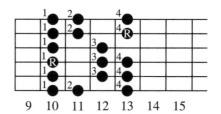

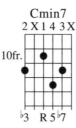

In **bar 69**, listen for the *call and response* between the piano and the guitar solo; one instrument states an idea, and the other responds. This is another basic yet tasteful technique for building a great solo. **Bar 81** has a cool descending-4ths lick drawn from the C Major scale fingering below. A study of this way of skipping through a scale in a specific interval will open the doors to new melodic ideas.

C Major Scale—8th Position

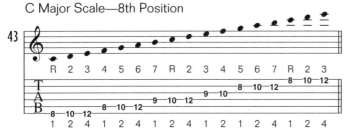

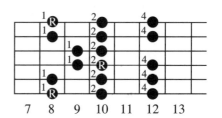

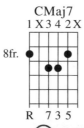

Entrances and Exits

Someone once said,

> " ... It's all about how you get in and get out,
> that's what the people remember most."

What that statement means is that you only get one entrance and one exit to your solo, so you better make them good. The entrance is where you get the audience interested enough to sit and listen to what you have to say on your guitar. The exit is where you leave them with a lasting impression.

The exit holds a little more weight. Imagine this scenario:

> You come in with the best line known to jazz, proceed to call upon the greats with all the well-practiced licks you lifted from solos on your favorite CDs, drive the band in and out of one great melody after the next, and effortlessly weave your way through a sophisticated palette of brilliant ideas. Oh yeah! There you are, tearing the roof off! People are dancing in the streets to your 13th chorus and you feel like you're just getting started. You are the beacon of swing, the defender of the jazz guitar universe, the king of bop! All eyes are now on you, you're stopping traffic, TV news crews are gathering, rock bands everywhere feel an eerie sensation that a new dawn is rising with every swing eighth you play. "Go! Go! Go! Go!" screams Jack Kerouac from afar. This is great! Blue Note is on their way down to sign you, you can't go wrong, life is peachy, RAD DUDE! YEAH, BABY, YEAH!...
>
> EEEEEERRRRRRKKKKKKK WHHAA BAM!!!!!
>
> ... oh man, you're last lick bombs. It just dies. It's over: the money, the fame, the cars, the mansion, the yacht...gone.

So here are a few ways to make sure your endings make front-page headlines for the *right* reasons:

- Repetition—Latch on to a catchy, memorable line and give it your all...over and over again!

- Dynamics—Approach the ending bars with a medium-volume run up the fretboard that ends with a loud, screaming bend which shatters every glass in the venue.

- Quoting—Simply bring the head back in, but with much more emotion, and don't be afraid to dress it up with only your finest embellishments.

Try mixing two or all of the above ideas into one incredible moment that will surely have the audience on their feet screaming for more. Listen to your favorite solos and ask yourself what it is about the entrances and exits that stick in your head. Whatever it is, it's all about how you get in and get out—that's what the people remember.

Solo 6

The Chart

"Peanut Butter and Gypsy Jam" is a 16-bar **AB** tune in A Minor in the style of a gypsy jazz standard called "Minor Swing." The head is played on the first chorus, followed by a three-chorus solo. The four-on-the-floor approach (with emphasis on beats 2 and 4) of this Django Reinhardt–inspired tune has similarities with the music of swing bands from the 1930s, such as the Count Basie Orchestra, which featured rhythm guitar pioneer Freddie Green.

- Though this tune is in a minor key, notice that the chords in **bars 1–4** of the **A** section are minor 6th (min6) chords. These chords give the tune a unique edge and may inspire some cool ideas for minor lines that you can carry over to more minor-7th oriented tunes.

- In **bar 6** of the **A** section, you will hear chromatic movement in the F7 to E7. This is yet another tritone substitution, but this time the tritone sub is the first of the two chords. The F7 is substituting for a B7, which would act as a V7 to E7. Also, listen for the second tritone sub in **bar 14** of the **B** section. The B♭7 is a sub for the preceding E7♭9, and they both set up the resolution to the tonic (Amin6).

- You will hear a rhythmic stomp, not so much driven by drums as it is from the guitar itself. This, and other styles that use this feel, are great for jamming with just another guitarist…or two, or three!

Have fun!

Django Reinhardt (1920–1953) recorded with the Quintet of the Hot Club of France in the 1930s. His recordings continue to have a strong influence on contemporary guitarists in many styles.

With Solo, Track 12
Backing Track, Track 13

Peanut Butter & Gypsy Jam Transcription

Transcribed by Johnny Buono

♩ = 196

Straight 8ths

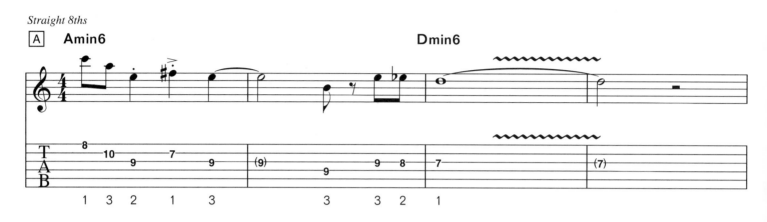

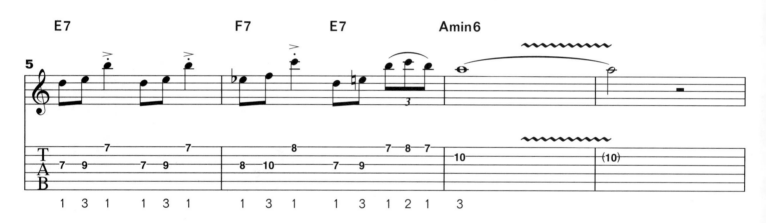

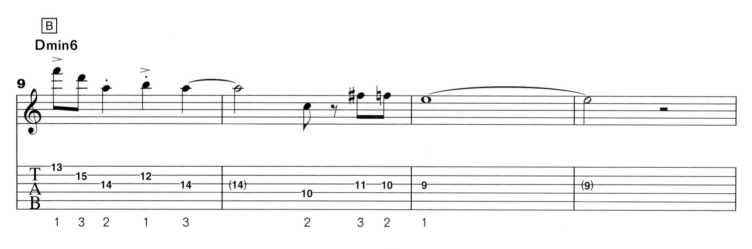

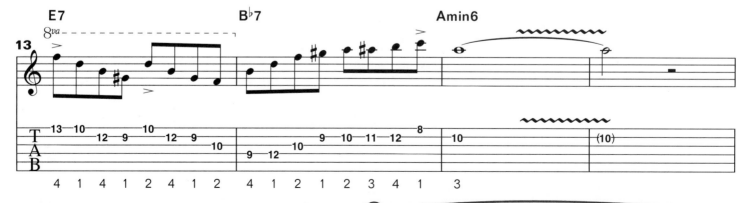

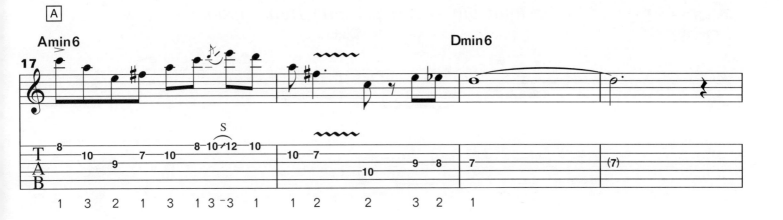

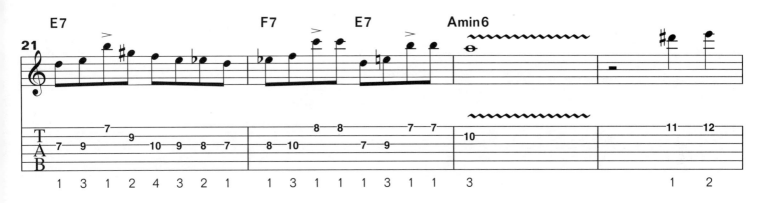

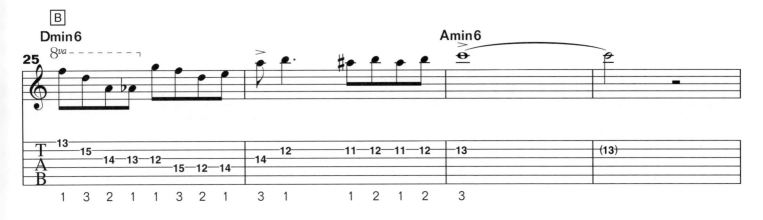

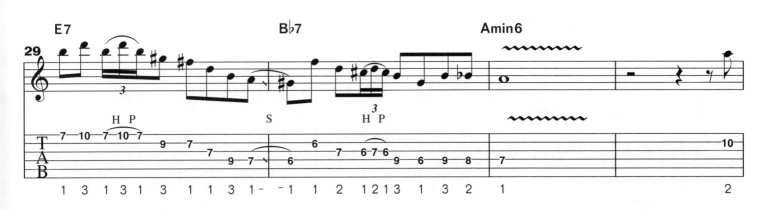

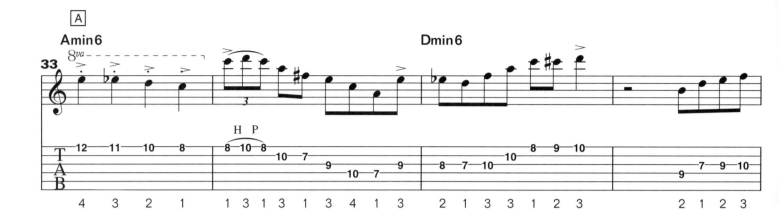

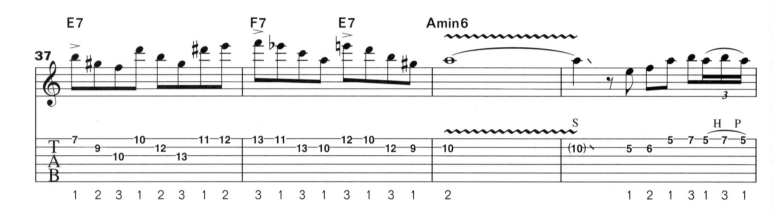

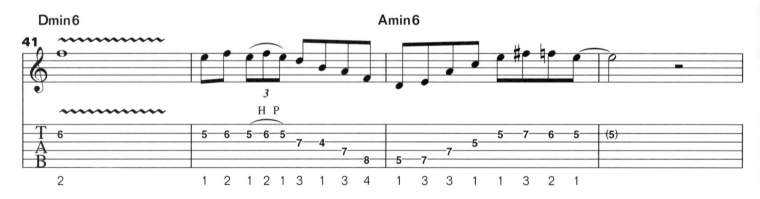

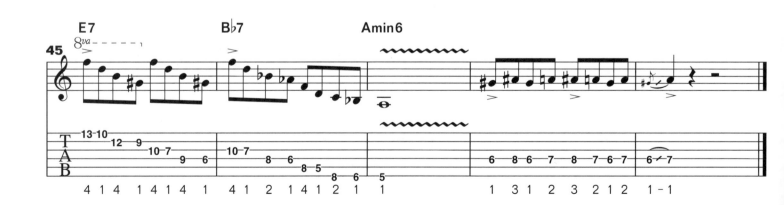

The Head

The "Peanut Butter and Gypsy Jam" head is mostly made up of arpeggio shapes. Learning the shapes below will not only help you understand how the head was embellished, but also provide a starting point for understanding how the solo ideas were constructed. Gypsy jazz soloists tend to stick more to arpeggio shapes and chromatic passing tones than to scale shapes.

Amin6 Arpeggio

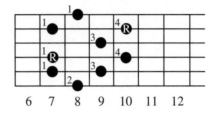
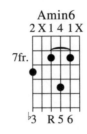

E7 Arpeggio Starting on B

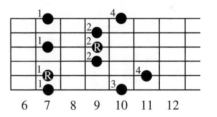
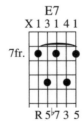

Dmin6 Arpeggio

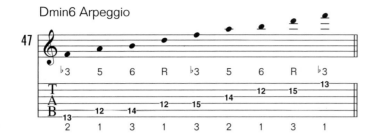

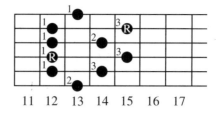

Dmin6

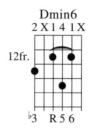

E7 Arpeggio Starting on E

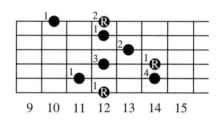

E7

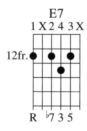

The Solo

Notice that as in the "Flipper Lane" solo (page 48), the head is reiterated in the second chorus where the improvising begins. Take a good listen to **bars 17–28** and you can clearly hear the head melody in the lines. This crucial technique cannot be stressed enough, and it's a guaranteed winner not just in jazz, but also in any other style of improvised music.

In **bar 45** you have a great shortcut for making dim7 arpeggios work as dominant 7♭9 arpeggios. Just play a dim7 arpeggio with a root one half step above the dominant 7 chord you're playing over, and you get the 7♭9 sound for that chord. Some *enharmonic* (notes that sound the same but have different names) respelling clarifies how this works. For example:

Fdim7 Creates a 7♭9 Sound Over E7

E7:
   E (root)
   G♯ (3)
   B (5)
   D (♭7)

Fdim7:
   F (♭9 of E7)
   A♭ (same as G♯, 3 of E7)
   C♭ (same as B, 5 of E7)
   E♭♭ (same as D, ♭7 of E7)

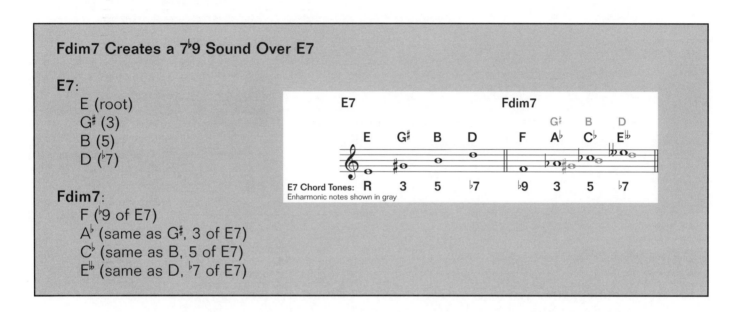

E7 Chord Tones: R 3 5 ♭7 ♭9 3 5 ♭7
Enharmonic notes shown in gray

By the way, this will work vertical wonders over that dim7 chord in bar 6 of "Johnny B. Blues Thing" on page 17. In the two examples that follow, you will see that the diminished 7 arpeggio is the same as the dominant 7 arpeggio, except the root has been raised a half step.

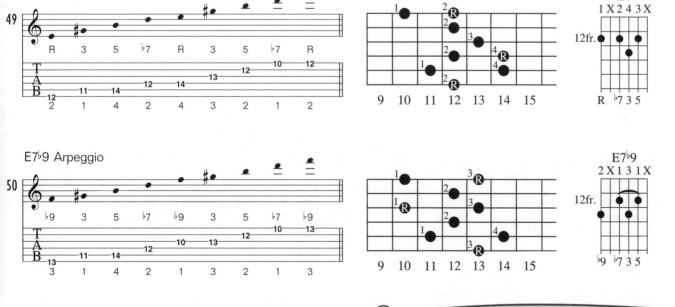

Approach Tones

One very important tool for jazz soloing is the use of *approach tones*, both *diatonic* (belonging to the key/scale) and *chromatic* (a half step away, not necessarily belonging to the key/scale). It could be as simple as preceding the *target note* (the note you're going for) with a note a half step above or below, or as intricate as surrounding the target note with several rising and falling half steps. Some examples of this technique in this solo are:

- **Bar 21**: The E♭ on beat 4 fills the gap between the chord tones that lead into the next vertical idea for F7.

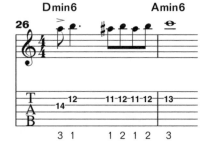

- **Bar 26**: This half-step lick builds some tension that resolves on the downbeat of bar 27.

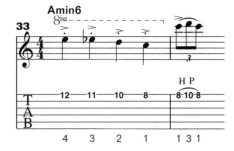

- **Bar 33**: The E♭ passing tone fills the gap for the bluesy walk down into the triplet in bar 34.

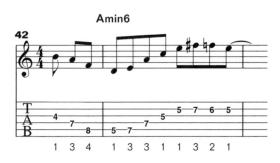

- **Bar 43**: The descending chromatic passage makes for a classy ending to the two-bar line that was started in bar 42 for the Dmin6–Amin6 change.

- **Bar 48**: The G♯ and A♯ surround the resolving root note (A) for an entire bar until finally ending the solo in bar 49.

A Rock Guy Asks a Jazz Cat: Q&A

Here are some answers to commonly asked questions about jazz and jazz soloing.

Rock Guy: *Dude, I don't have one of those big grandpa* [hollow body archtop] *guitars, but I got this rockin' custom-made, Ultra-Mega Metal GAS662 model with the smoke machine. Can I still jam with you?*

Jazz Cat: Dig this my man, it don't matter if you come down to jam with a full-blown, beautifully handmade jazz box by the finest Italian builder money can buy, or a ukulele. As long as you can play and you got something to say on the instrument, it don't matter what you got. Besides, there are plenty of big-name jazz guitar cats that do not exclusively play with a hollow-body, such as: Pat Martino, Mike Stern, Pat Metheny, John Mclaughlin and Al Di Meola.

RG: *Dude, what's with the drummer? No double kick drum, no china cymbals, not even roto-toms. And, uh, does this guy know what's he's doing? He was like, all over the place.*

JC: My man, just because you don't hear boom–kah, boom–boom–kah, doesn't mean you need to get upset. Jazz is always in motion, and every player drives it in the moment in which it is played. The drummer is speaking a spatial language that enables the group to *flow* through the tune like water. By the way, good jazz drummers can play the floor tiles if they have to.

RG: *Yo, I played with one of those bass players who have the bass you spin around, but I didn't get it. He played so many notes I got lost!*

JC: [*chuckle*] Actually, he's the guy you should listen to when you *get* lost! Man, it's okay to be confused at first, and a little scared of an upright acoustic bass. The cat is only laying in the pocket and outlining the chords for you to blow over.

RG: *Okay, dude, one more. How do you know when the next guy is going to take the next rippin' solo with all those notes that sound wrong* [wink and a smile]?

JC: Well, it goes like this. The band starts in on the head, which is usually played by the bandleader. If the leader is a drummer, the others will talk it over before the gig and divvy up the tunes. Sometimes they will even make a solo order. After the head, the first player takes his solo, does his thing, and then he gives some kind of signal that he's nearing the end. A nod or a wave of the hand usually does it. The next cat on deck gets ready to blow, and when the time comes, they both weave in out of each other's solo entrance and exit. This flow grooves on until the last solo is played and then you got to give the drummer some. Usually the drummer will *trade fours, [alternate four-bar solos]* with the other players until the chart evens out to the beginning and it's time to play the head again. After the head is played, sometimes the leader, or the featured soloist, will take an *outro [ending]* solo over a chord *vamp [short, repeated series of chords]* and then give the nod to end the tune when he's ready.

Solo 7

The Chart

"Bossa Rhymes" is another 16-bar **AB** chart, this time using a *Latin* (South American, usually Brazilian) feel. The tune consists of a one-chorus head followed by a two-chorus solo. This C Minor chart is in the style of the famous Kenny Dorham tune, *Blue Bossa.* Like "Peanut Butter & Gypsy Jazz" and "Rodney's Groove," "Bossa Rhymes" departs from the swing feel of the other charts and takes on its own unique rhythmic flow. This chart is traditionally a jazz guitarist's introduction to the bossa nova style pioneered by the great composer Antonio Carlos Jobim.

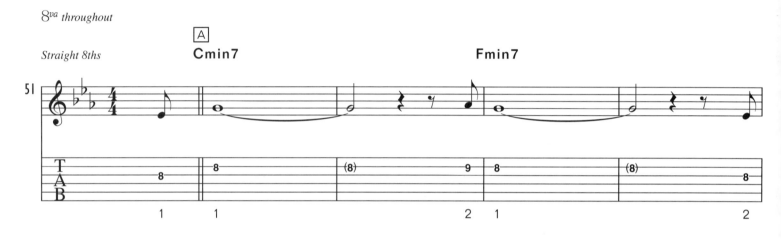

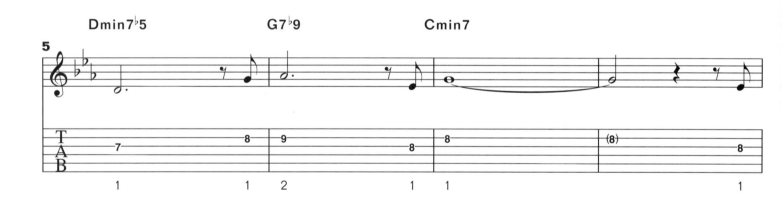

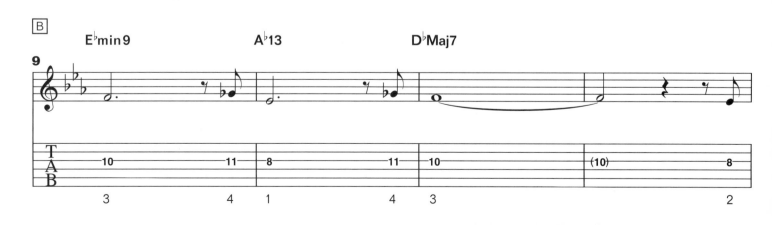

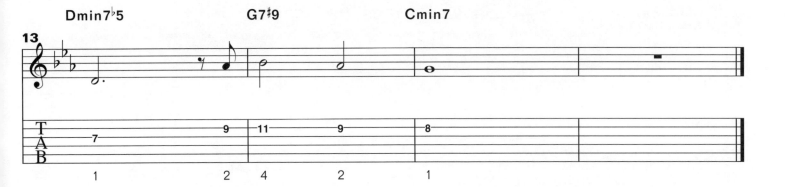

- Listen for the ii–Vs in **bars 5 and 6** of the **A** section and **bars 13 and 14** of the **B** section. Both ii–Vs can be heard as either harmonic minor or melodic minor changes (that is, the harmonies could come from either scale).

- Check out the cool half-step modulation up to the key of D♭ Major in **bars 9–12** of the **B** section. A good way to learn how to solo over changing key centers is to practice over only one key at a time, and then go back and put them together a few at a time, until you can get through them all.

- Notice the tricky Cuban carnival rhythm employed by the rhythm section, which adds even more to the Latin sound.

Baden Powell *(1937–2000) was, perhaps, Brazil's greatest guitarist and a famed composer of samba and bossa. He was born in Rio and lived in Europe for many years .*

Bossa Rhymes Transcription

Transcribed by Steve Hager

♩ = 134

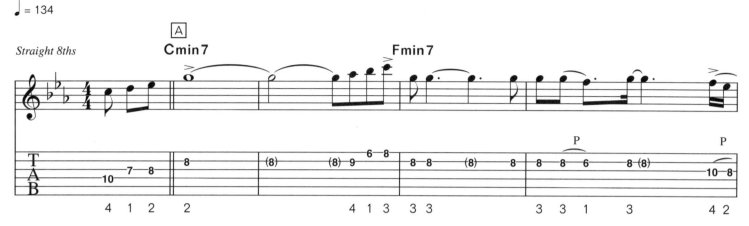

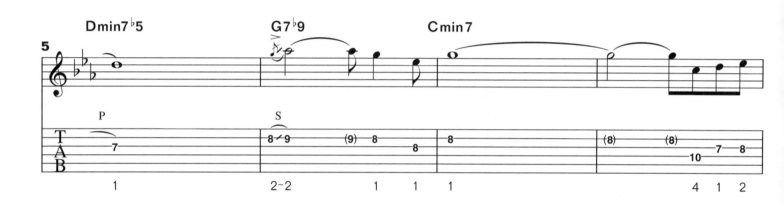

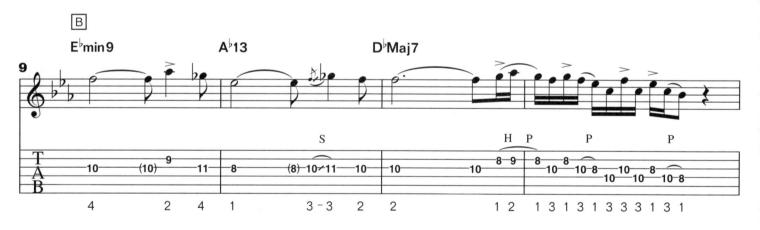

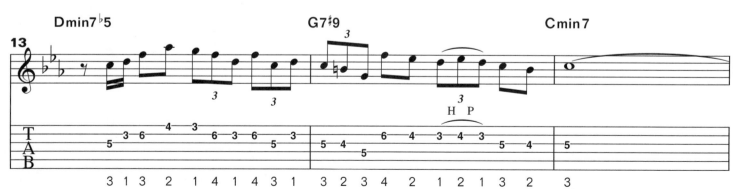

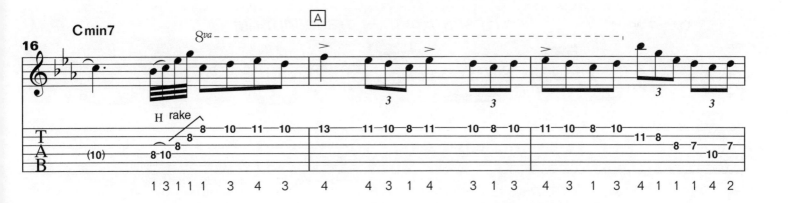

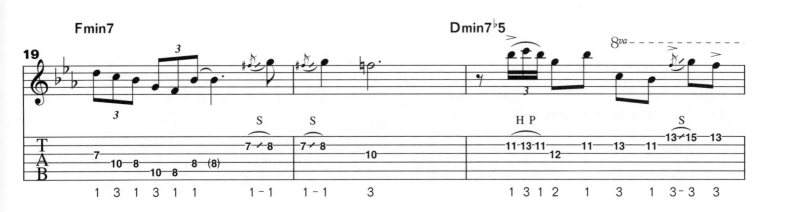

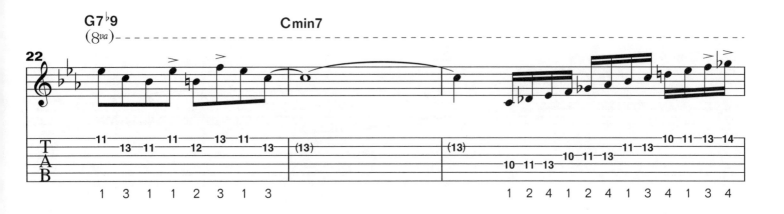

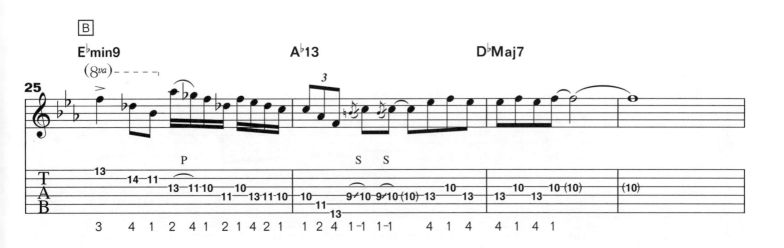

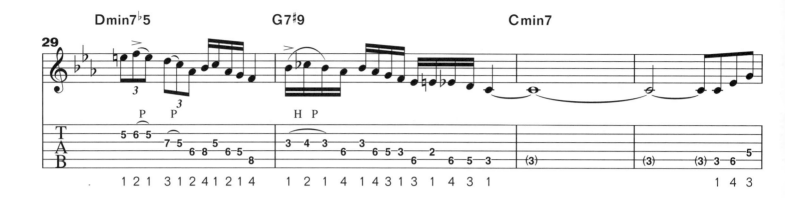

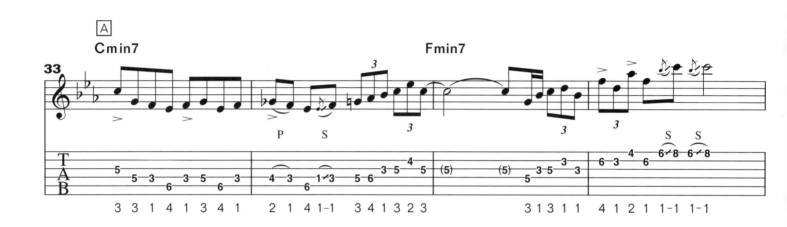

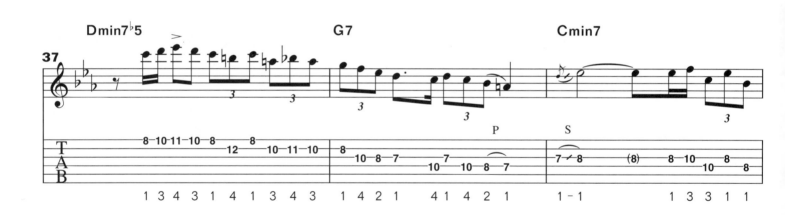

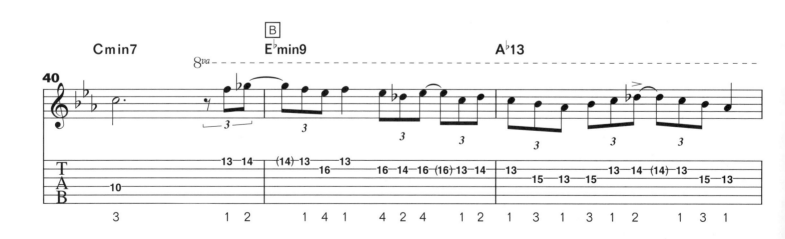

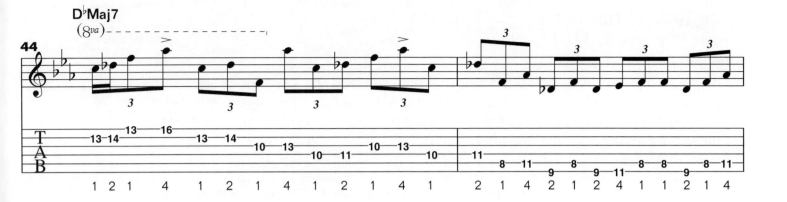

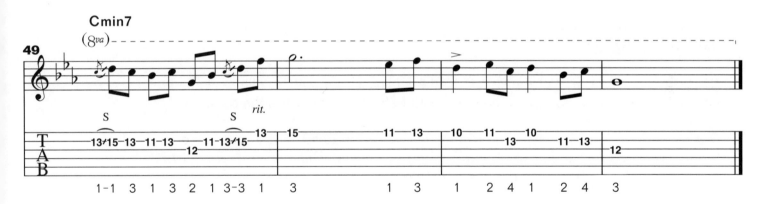

The Head

"Bossa Rhymes" has a simple head that incorporates the concept of multiple *pickup notes* (notes occurring before the first full measure of a tune or phrase). The head was enhanced in the solo with additional notes played in front of those pick-ups with varying rhythms characteristic of Latin phrasing, such as quarter-note triplets.

Improvising a completely new melody, as opposed to what is written on the chart, is a liberty that should be approached with care and respect for the tune and its composer. In **bar 13** you will hear an improvised line that was substituted for the head. This worked because it followed and matched another improvised line for the D♭Maj7 chord in **bar 11**, and set the tone for the solo.

The Solo

One of the most overlooked components of a great jazz solo is *dynamics* (varying degrees of loudness and softness). Your lines need to have this element or they will sound bland and one dimensional. Dynamics will also keep you from getting lost in the mix.

For examples of the use of dynamics, check out these bars in the recording (follow along with the chart).

Bars 16–20 open the solo with a dramatic intro line that is loaded with accents. Notice the *rake* in **bar 17**. This is done by sweeping the pick in one motion across the top four strings.

Bar 24 has a nice run over the Cmin7 to the E♭min9 chord, and its climax is made obvious by the louder notes as it finishes (right before resolving into the downbeat).

Bar 40 starts a long line that journeys all the way to the end of the tune. One of the key reasons this line is so effective is the dynamics, which have a number of peaks and valleys. Listen for these key moments:

- The line comes in at a medium volume at **bar 40**. It slowly gets softer, only to peak at the high 16th-fret A♭.

- Then the line gets softer again for the long descending D♭Maj7 arpeggio in **bar 44**.

- It again rises in volume as the notes climb up the Dmin7♭5 arpeggio in **bar 46**.

- The line continues to "breathe" in and out until the resolution in **bar 49**.

In **bars 29 and 30** you can hear another approach to playing vertically over a ii–V. Below are the fingerings for the D Locrian ♮2 and G Altered scales used to play that line. Don't forget to transpose these licks to all keys so they are readily available for any given tune.

D Locrian Mode

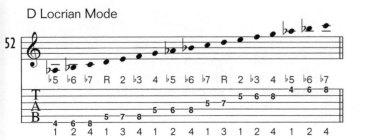

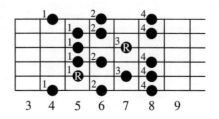

Dmin7♭5

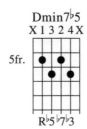

G Altered Scale

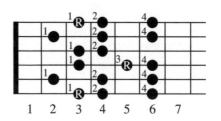

G7♯5♯9

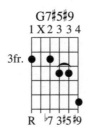

Here are the fingerings for the D♭Maj7 and Dmin7♭5 arpeggios for playing vertically in **bars 43–45**. Notice that the lick in bar 45, derived from the Dmin7♭5 arpeggio, is played without the C (♭7), making it a D diminished triad. The fingering for the Dmin7♭5 arpeggio below has the C in parentheses, but the whole fingering is there so you can see it as a Dmin7♭5 to match the chord over which it is played.

D♭Maj7 Arpeggio

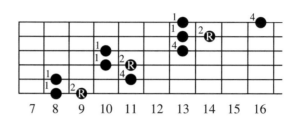

D♭Maj7
1 X 3 4 2 X

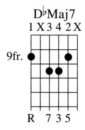

9fr.

R 7 3 5

Dmin7♭5 Arpeggio

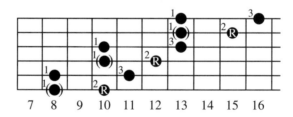

Dmin7♭5
2 X 3 4 1 X

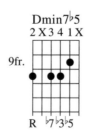

9fr.

R ♭7 ♭3 ♭5

Storytellers

Do you want the *real*, real deal about how to build a great jazz solo? It involves you not playing a single note!

That's right, not a one; you just need to listen. Listen to as many jazz artists as your ears, mind and neighbors can handle. Listening to jazz is an essential part of learning to play jazz.

Since playing a great jazz solo is like telling a good story, it only makes sense that you should listen to how stories are told by some master storytellers. Here are a select few to check out:

Guitar	*Other*
George Benson	Louis Armstrong, *trumpet*
Lenny Breau	John Coltrane, *tenor sax*
Charlie Christian	Chick Corea, *piano/keyboards*
Tal Farlow	Miles Davis, *trumpet*
David Fiuczynski	Eric Dolphy, *alto sax, flute, clarinet*
Bill Frisell	Duke Ellington, *piano, band leader*
Freddie Green	Bill Evans, *piano*
Grant Green	Ella Fitzgerald, *singer*
Jim Hall	Dizzy Gillespie, *trumpet*
Vic Juris	Herbie Hancock, *piano/keyboards*
Wayne Krantz	Billie Holiday, *singer*
Pat Martino	Keith Jarrett, *piano*
John McLaughlin	Rashaan Roland Kirk, *tenor sax, flute, etc.*
Pat Metheny	Charles Mingus, *bass*
Wes Montgomery	Charlie Parker, *alto sax*
Joe Pass	Sonny Rollins, *tenor sax*
Django Reinhardt	Wayne Shorter, *tenor sax*

Some of these names may unfamiliar, but to jazz cats in the know, these are giants, old and new, who have written the stories you should be learning.

Solo 8

The Chart

"Modal Lava" is the final solo in this book. It is a 32-bar **AABA** arrangement in the D Dorian mode. The tune runs through the head on the first chorus and then goes into a three-chorus solo, which then continues into a long vamp on the **A** section. Don't be fooled by the lack of chords in this tune, the trick here is to keep your place without getting lost, especially at this tempo! Classic examples of this style can be found in Miles Davis' "So What" and John Coltrane's "Impressions." The head is shown below.

8ᵛᵃ throughout

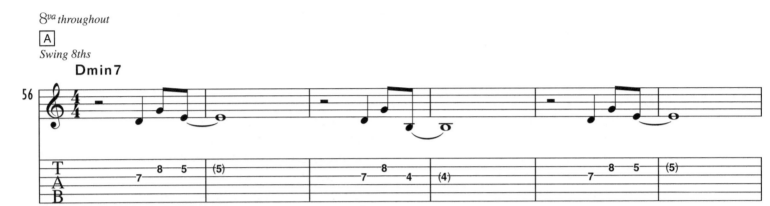

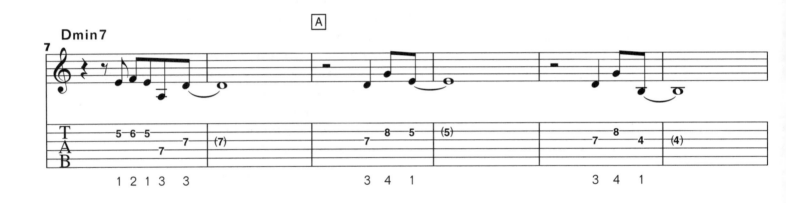

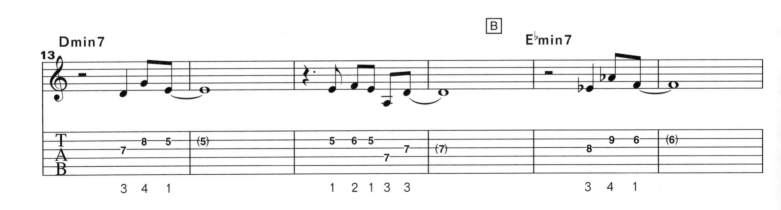

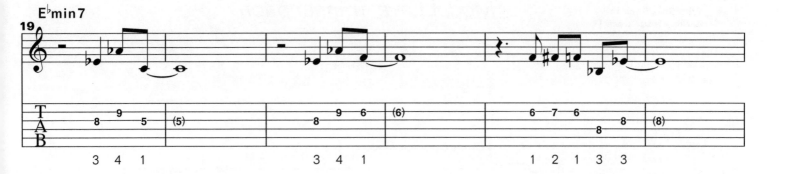

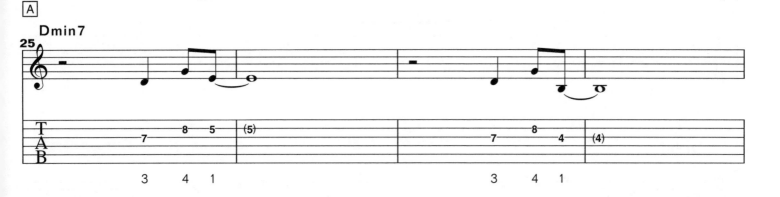

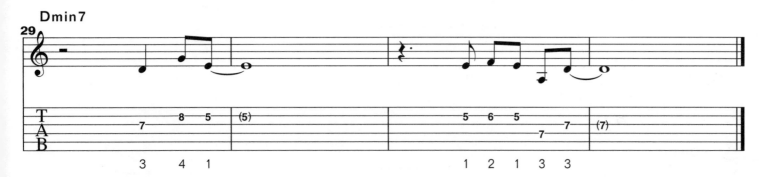

- Listen to track 17, the version without the guitar solo, and try these ideas to help you learn how to keep your place:

   1. Count the beats aloud while saying the measure number at the beginning of each bar, like this, **1**–2–3–4, **2**–2–3–4, **3**–2–3–4, and so on.

   2. Listen for a cue from any instrument as to when an eight-bar section has been played through. It could be a cymbal crash, an accented piano chord, or a resolution from a climactic bass line into the downbeat of the next section.

- Try not to be overwhelmed by the fast tempo. Just relax, keep your lines simple at first, use space to your advantage, and most of all, have fun!

Modal Lava Transcription

Transcribed by Doug Osborn

♩ = 134

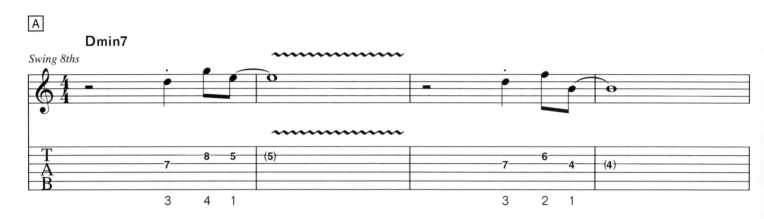

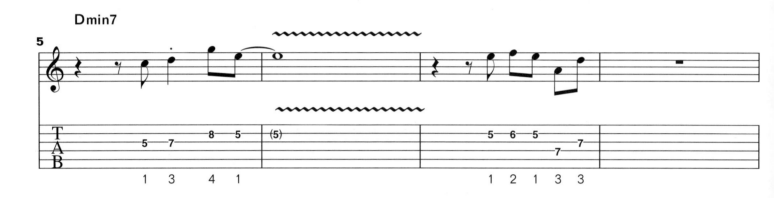

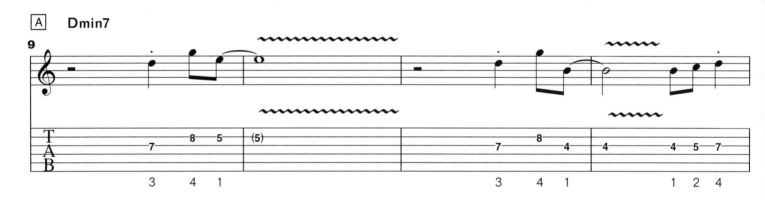

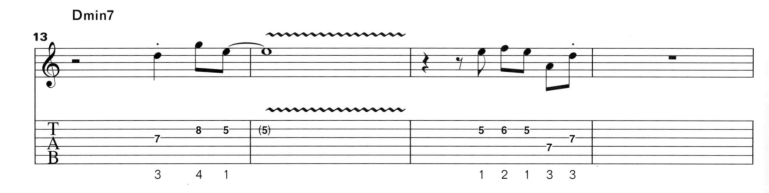

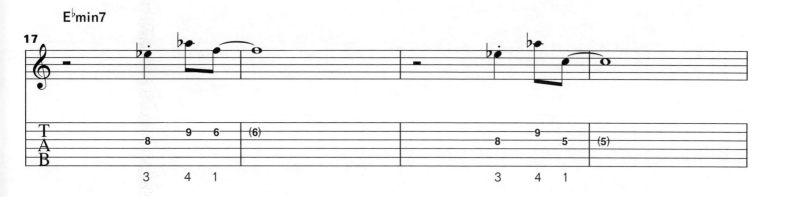

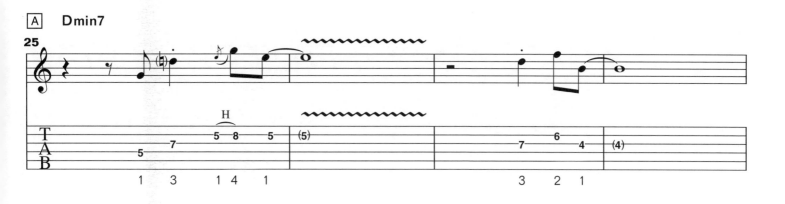

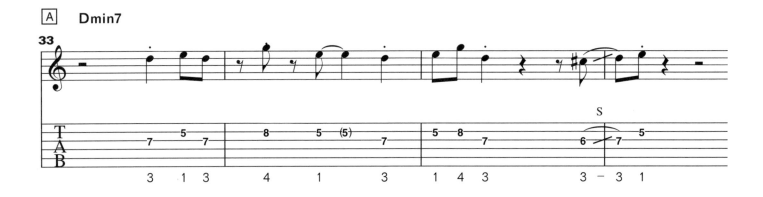

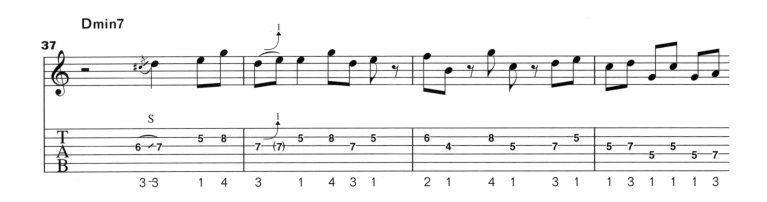

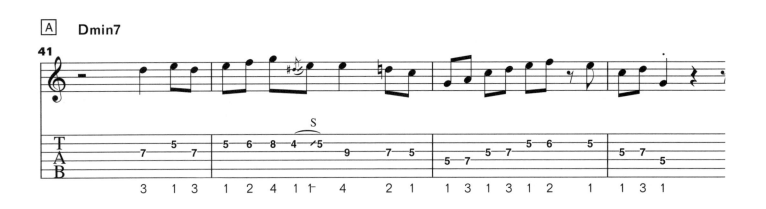

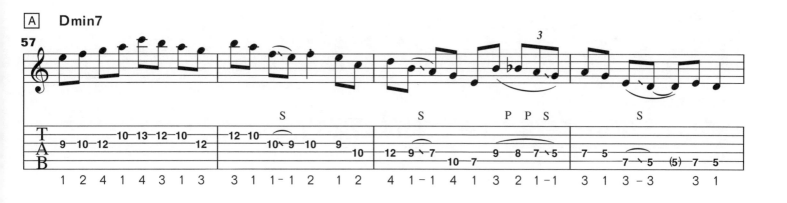

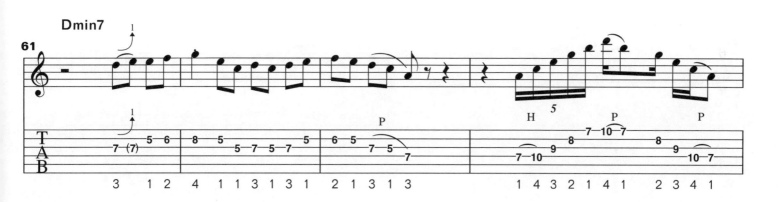

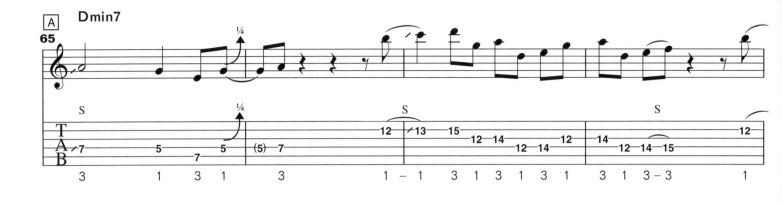

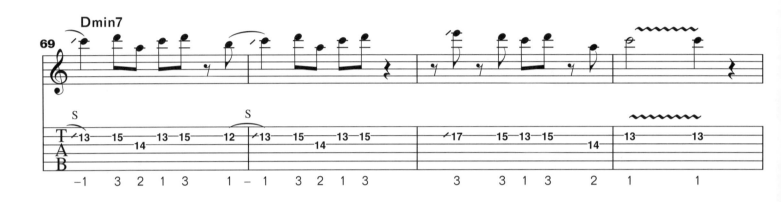

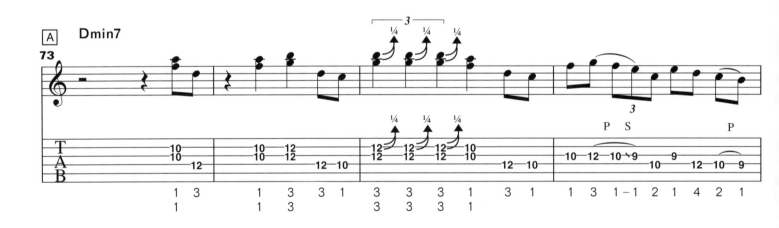

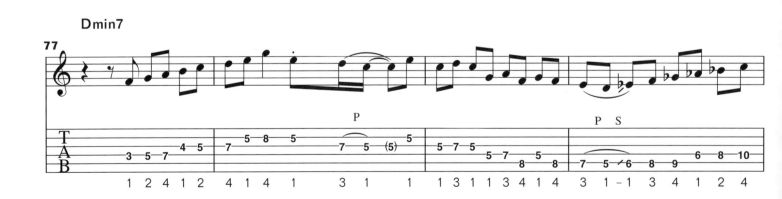

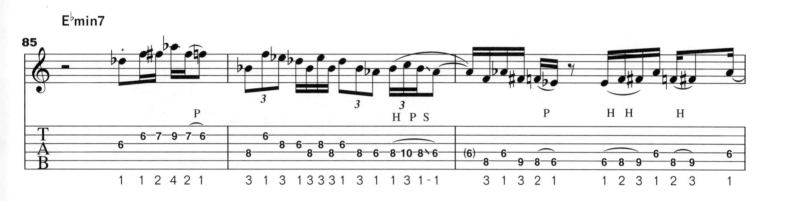

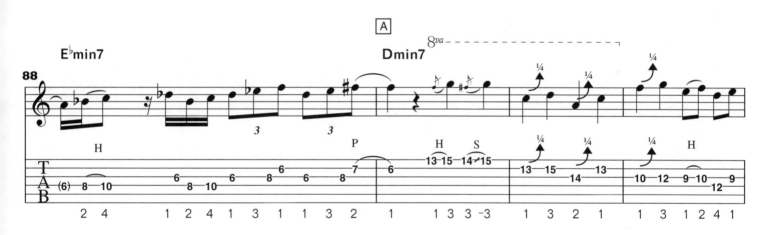

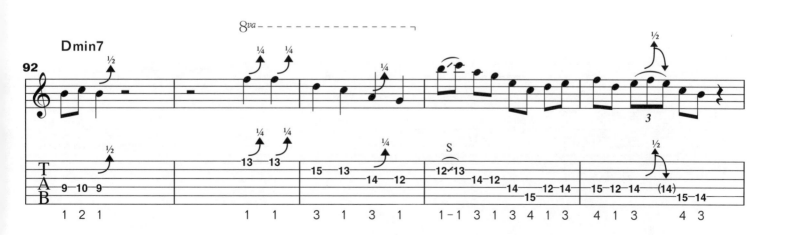

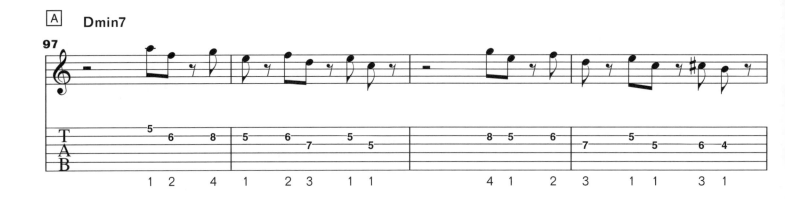

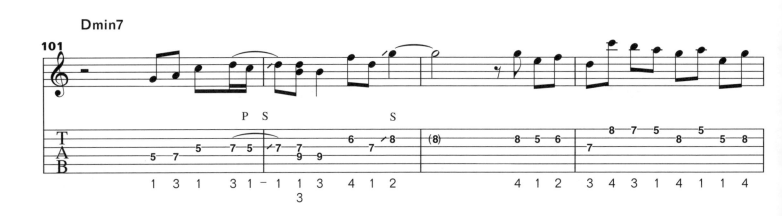

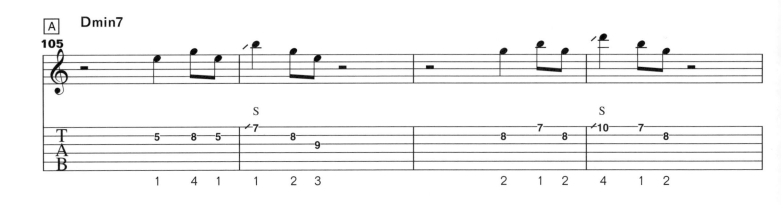

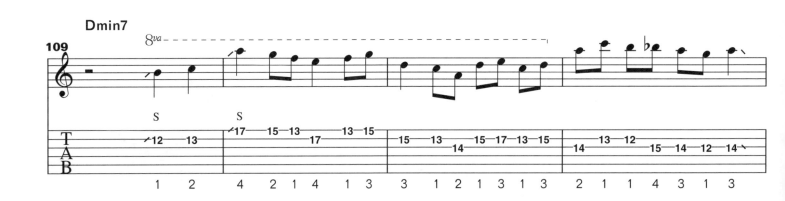

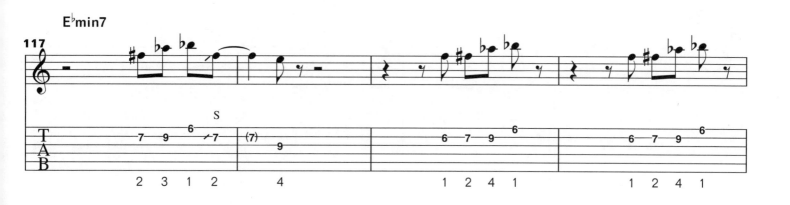

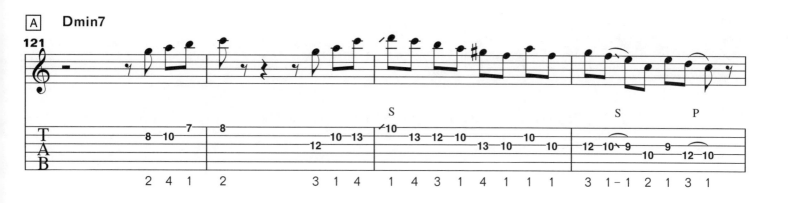

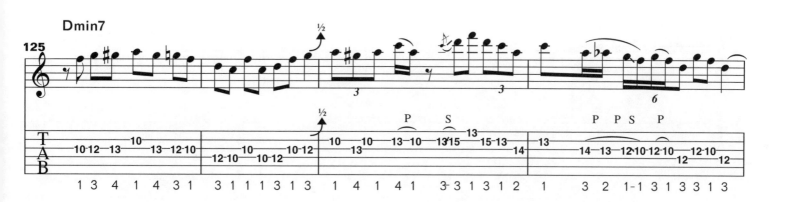

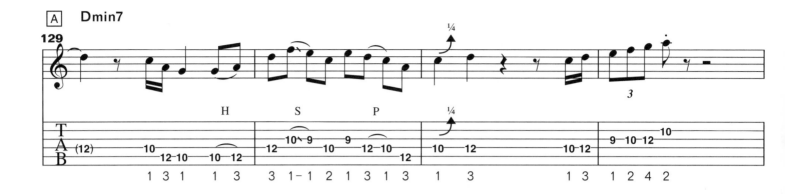

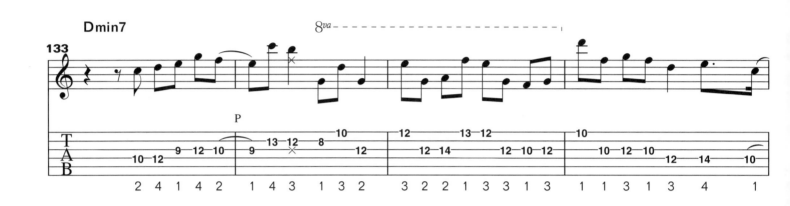

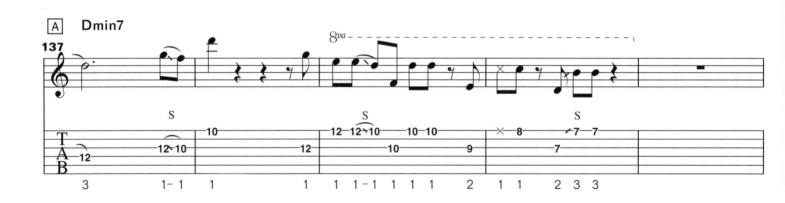

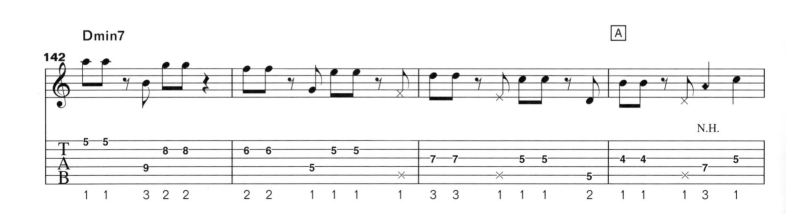

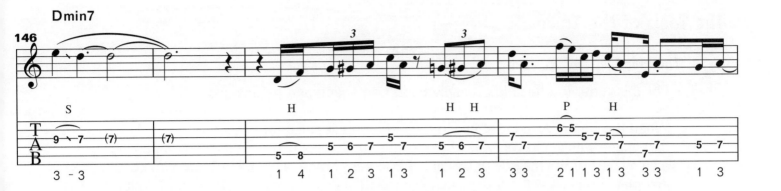

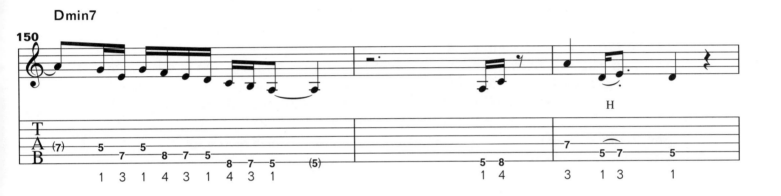

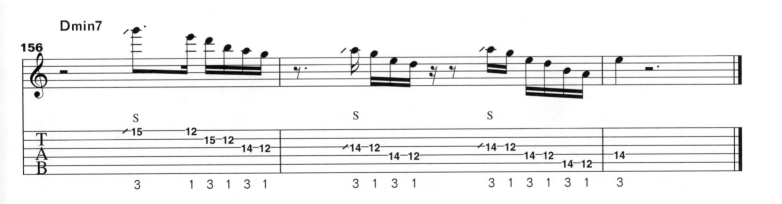

The Head

For this tune, the head is primarily based on space and extensions.

When the head has a lot of space between phrases, it's up to you to tastefully fill that space with whatever works best for the tune. It could be as simple as repeating a small part of the melody or building a counter phrase, as in **bar 12**. Or, you could just play the head without *any* embellishments and just concentrate on putting it in the pocket.

The Solo

As mentioned earlier on page 78, the fact that there are only two chords in the entire tune doesn't mean you can't lose your place. In fact, it may happen more easily! Organizing your ideas can prevent this from happening. For example, in this solo, listen to the way there is a theme to each eight-bar section and to each chorus as a whole. Also, listen for those exciting, climatic lines that end all three full choruses. Don't miss the call and response lines in **bars 89–96**. All of these components are used to organize the solo into a cohesive story for the listener, and to make it easier for the rhythm section to follow. This is also a great way for you keep your place!

The solo starts with short melodic passages and rhythmic variations in **bar 33** that are purposefully referring to the head. This technique is known as *quoting*. The D Dorian scale below was used for the lines in **bars 33–45** as well as many other spots in the solo, such as **bars 61–63, 78–79, 97–108** and **142–150**.

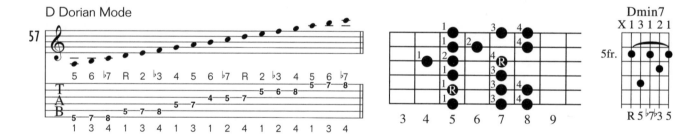

Now simply take the above D Dorian scale and its matching chord shape, and move it up a half step and you have the E♭ Dorian fingering and matching chord shape used for the lines in **bars 81–88** of the second chorus and **bars 113–120** of the third chorus.

The remaining tools are for the first chorus E♭min7 change. After the first line, which uses the Dorian fingering from page 90 (up one half step), the solo continues for **bars 50–53** in E♭ Minor and uses the two scales below to create a lick that travels down the fretboard. This makes a Dorian roadmap that ends in **bar 54** with yet another visit to the Dorian fingering from page 90 (again, up one half step).

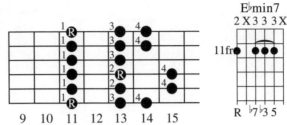

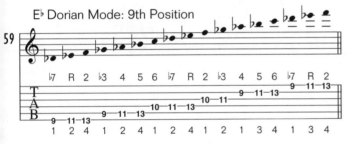

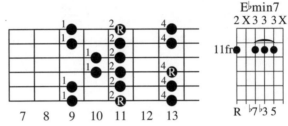

Check out the two important D Dorian scale fingerings below. Watch for the first one in **bars 67–71**, **89 and 90**, **93–96** and **109–112**. The next scale is used in **bars 123–124** and **129–139**.

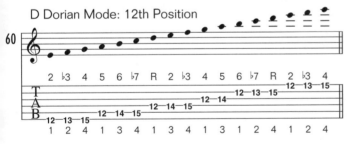

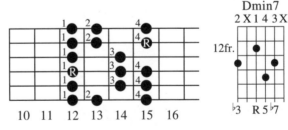

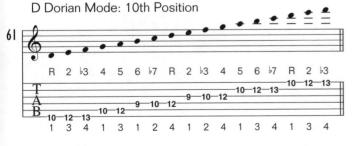

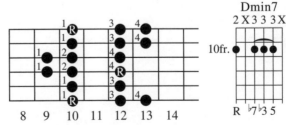

In **bars 125–128** you will find the D Minor Blues scale below.

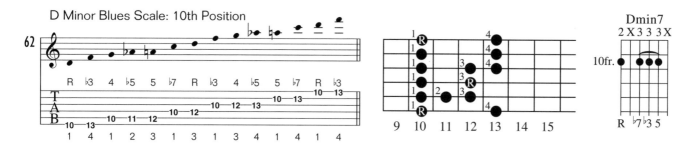

D Minor Blues Scale: 10th Position

Dmin7

The next D Minor Blues scale starts the tour de force ending vamp in **bar 148**.

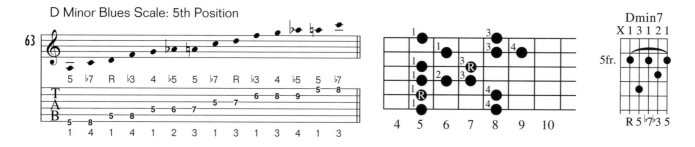

D Minor Blues Scale: 5th Position

Dmin7

To finish things off, the two A Minor Pentatonic scales below were superimposed over Dmin starting in **bar 151** through to the end.

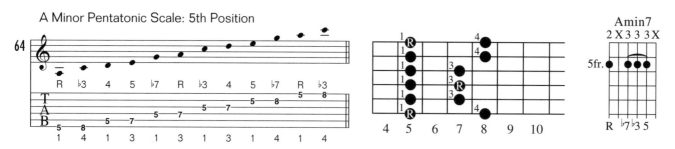

A Minor Pentatonic Scale: 5th Position

Amin7

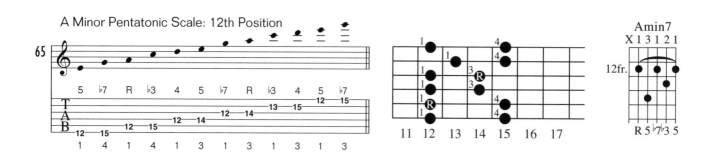

A Minor Pentatonic Scale: 12th Position

Amin7

Below is a list of some intermediate to advanced techniques found in this solo that are sure to catch an audience by surprise.

- In **bar 64**, the more laid-back first chorus comes to a thrilling close as a result of the *sweep picking* employed for the CMaj9 arpeggio which is superimposed over the Dmin sound. Sweep picking is an economical technique that incorporates a single stroke across the strings with a uniform picking direction (either up or down). This works especially well with arpeggios and other melodic ideas that have one note per string (or two notes using hammer-ons or pull-offs).

- In a few choice spots, there is some bending. Check out **bars 38, 61, 84, 92, 96, 126, and 155**. Though bending might be more associated with rock and blues, jazz musicians are always drawing influences and inspirations from a limitless pool of musical styles.

- For the rapid lines in **bars 85–88, 127–128** and **148–150**, you will need to become familiar with *hybrid picking*. This technique uses the right-hand middle finger in conjunction with a conventional picking style. The right-hand ring and pinky fingers can also be used together or separately. Normally found in country and bluegrass guitar playing, hybrid picking allows us to play lines that have wide interval leaps and rapid string changes at rapid tempos. It can also help us put in accents that would otherwise be very difficult to perform.

The Real Deal

Parting Words

Hopefully, the solos and lessons in this book have given you what you need to build great jazz guitar solos and have lots of fun doing it. Now it's your job to practice using the tools of the trade you have learned, get a band together and *play*!

Addendum

Here are the scales and modes used in the solos in this book:

AEOLIAN

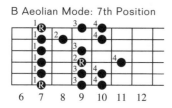

B Aeolian Mode: 7th Position

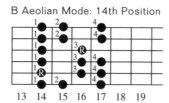

B Aeolian Mode: 14th Position

DORIAN

D Dorian Mode: 5th Position

C Dorian Mode: 10th Position

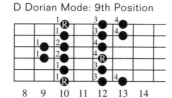

D Dorian Mode: 9th Position

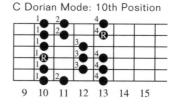

D Dorian Mode: 12th Position

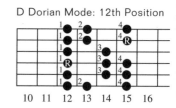

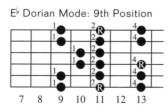

E♭ Dorian Mode: 9th Position

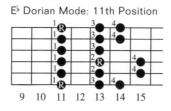

E♭ Dorian Mode: 11th Position

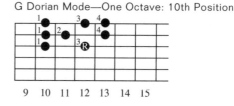

G Dorian Mode—One Octave: 10th Position

MAJOR

The B♭ Major scale fingerings were also used for the relative minor, G Minor.

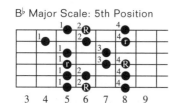

B♭ Major Scale: 5th Position

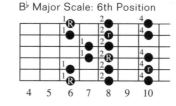

B♭ Major Scale: 6th Position

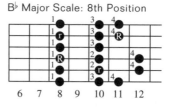

B♭ Major Scale: 8th Position

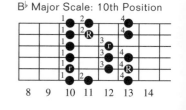

B♭ Major Scale: 10th Position

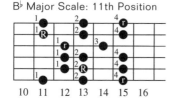

B♭ Major Scale: 11th Position

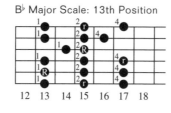

B♭ Major Scale: 13th Position

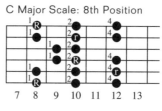

C Major Scale: 8th Position

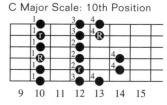

C Major Scale: 10th Position

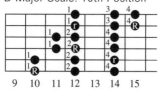

D Major Scale: 10th Position

MAJOR PENTATONIC, MAJOR AND MINOR BLUES

F Major Pentatonic Scale:
10th Position

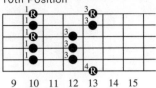

9 10 11 12 13 14 15

B♭ Major Blues Scale:
6th Position

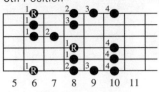

5 6 7 8 9 10 11

F Major Blues Scale:
8th Position

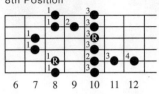

6 7 8 9 10 11 12

D Minor Blues Scale:
5th Position

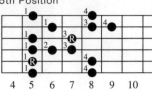

4 5 6 7 8 9 10

D Minor Blues Scale:
10th Position

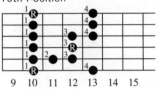

9 10 11 12 13 14 15

G Minor Blues Scale:
3rd Position

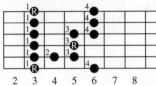

2 3 4 5 6 7 8

MINOR PENTATONIC

A Minor Pentatonic Scale:
5th Position

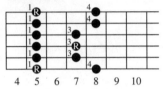

4 5 6 7 8 9 10

A Minor Pentatonic Scale:
7th Position

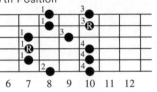

6 7 8 9 10 11 12

A Minor Pentatonic Scale:
12th Position

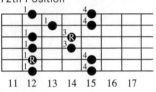

11 12 13 14 15 16 17

B Minor Pentatonic Scale:
7th Position

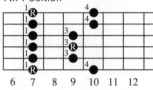

6 7 8 9 10 11 12

B Minor Pentatonic Scale:
9th Position

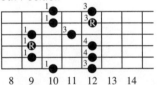

8 9 10 11 12 13 14

C Minor Pentatonic Scale:
3rd Position

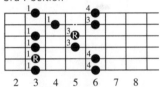

2 3 4 5 6 7 8

G Minor Pentatonic Scale:
3rd Position

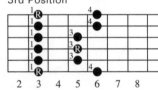

2 3 4 5 6 7 8

G Minor Pentatonic Scale:
5th Position

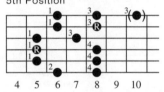

4 5 6 7 8 9 10

MIXOLYDIAN AND MIXOLYDIAN ♭9

D Mixolydian Mode—One Octave:
7th Position

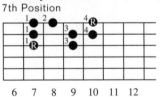

6 7 8 9 10 11 12

D Mixolydian ♭9 Mode:
7th Position

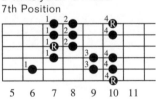

5 6 7 8 9 10 11

B♭ Mixolydian Scale—One Octave:
13th Position

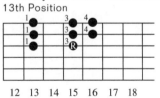

12 13 14 15 16 17 18

OTHER MODES AND SCALES

D Locrian Mode:
4th Position

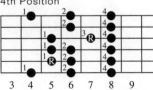

3 4 5 6 7 8 9

E♭ Lydian Mode—One Octave:
8th Position

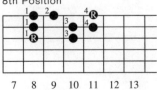

7 8 9 10 11 12 13

G Altered Scale:
2nd Position

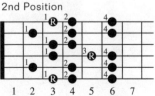

1 2 3 4 5 6 7

G Altered Scale:
4th Position

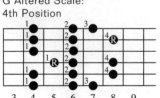

3 4 5 6 7 8 9